Biblical

Dream Symbols

Dictionary

2nd Edition

A-Z

Includes Numbers and Colors

Tyler Wolfe

For the Saints in Christ, whom I dearly love

Contents

Preface

There are many books available on how to interpret dreams, but few dedicated to the collection and interpretation of the symbols. This dictionary was written to satisfy that void. I have interpreted thousands of dreams in the practice of evangelism and I update my reference material based on those encounters. As such, the second edition of the Biblical Dream Symbols Dictionary is a revision and expansion of the first after much clinical use.

Tyler Wolfe

The Interpretation of Dreams

Where do dreams come from?

The Bible teaches that dreams originate from three different sources: a person's soul, God and demons. Isaiah 29:8 gives us an example of a dream originating from the soul as a response to extreme hunger. These dreams are a normal biological process thought to consolidate old memories, relieve us of stress or fulfill repressed desires. Because these dreams come from our flesh, they can appear random and difficult to understand (Jer. 17:9).

The second source of our dreams is demonic spirits. Jeremiah 27:9 gives us an example of dreams with a demonic origin. There we see "dreamers" listed with false prophecy, fortune-telling and sorcery. The Bible teaches that these activities are caused by demons (Jer. 23:13, Acts 16:16). Placing dreamers in the context of this list establishes them as being inspired by demons as well. Another example can be found in Job 2:6. There we are told that Satan is the culprit of Job's trouble including the death of his family and the loss of his property. When Job goes on to say he is suffering from terrifying dreams (Job 7:14), it is logical to conclude that Satan is the cause.

The third source of our dreams is God. The prophet Daniel calls a dream from God a "true" dream (Dan. 2:45). Daniel does this as a way of distinguishing it from dreams that come from other sources. A true dream is inspired by the Holy Spirit as a way to instruct us. God wants people to understand these types of dreams (Job 33:14-16).

What is a God-given dream?

Dreams can be used as a form of communication based on a system of symbols. A symbol serves as a representation of a thought. People need to see and hear in order for something to make sense and to fully comprehend. God asked the prophets to act out His messages to Israel so that by seeing, the people would better understand them (Ezek. 12:1-7, Jer. 13:1-11). Dreams communicate meaning in the same way as the prophetic message.

Symbols act on the emotional and intuitive side of human beings to bring meaning to our lives. In the purest sense, a God-given dream is an allegorical play; a story that uses extensive symbolism. A God-given dream is intended for instruction and includes literary features like plot, setting, characters and the viewpoint of the narrator. Many times the narrator (God) will clearly express to us the meaning of the dream by using a summary statement at the end.

Why does God use dreams to communicate?

Communication is an attempt to transfer knowledge from one individual to another. In certain forms of communication this is done through the use of constructs and concepts; both represent objects of thought.

Communication exists when those communicating agree upon the meaning of the symbols and gestures being used. Agreeing upon a definition is not always adequate to produce effective communication. Non-verbal, spoken, written and signed communication is not an exact representation of an object of thought. Our understanding is diminished by the limits of received language.

The reason God uses dreams is because images communicate meaning more effectively than written or spoken language. In essence, God is showing you pictures of what He wants to say.

How should a Christian interpret dreams?

Christians should approach dream analysis with an understanding of the literary theory of authorial intent. For the purpose of dream interpretation authorial intent means that the author encoded the meaning into the dream. If God is the author of the dream then He alone gets to determine the meaning. The only way of accurately deciphering the meaning of a God-given dream is by defining the symbols using the Bible. The symbols by themselves cannot interpret your dream. The overall context of the dream provides continuity between the symbols. Ultimately, it is the unction of the Holy Spirit that articulates an accurate interpretation of any dream.

Common dream themes

1. Flying. In Jer. 48:9 the Bible equates having wings with the ability to move swiftly. In this sense, flying can symbolize an uncommon freedom over your circumstances in life. Flying is also indicative of having total control in a situation or having little resistance in all of your endeavors.

2. Falling. The Bible says in Prov. 11:14 that a lack of guidance causes people to fall. The sensation of falling may reveal a lack of Godly wisdom and guidance in your life or not having control over your circumstances. Watching other people fall in a dream is also common and symbolizes a perspective over the dangers in other people's lives.

3. Pregnancy. To dream of being pregnant can symbolize an unborn idea, job, project or major change in a person's life. Pregnancy symbolizes the implantation or seeding of a new thing into a person's life. The Bible says in Isa. 42:9 that God will declare new things to you before they spring forth. A pregnancy dream can also be a prophetic announcement from God concerning the conception of a child. Not all pregnancy dreams are from God. An ungodly idea may also manifest itself as a pregnancy dream.

4. Birth. Giving birth is similar to a pregnancy dream in that it is the fulfillment of the promise of a new thing in your life. Many times people can dream of giving birth to multiple children. This is symbolic of a series of new things. At times grown men alarmingly dream of giving birth. In a birth dream the child may be born as a toddler or an adolescent symbolic of the unusual maturity of the new thing in your life. Conversely, a child may be born emaciated or elderly, complete with grey hair, missing teeth and wrinkled skin. This is symbolic of the premature death or inability of the dreamer to sustain the vitality of the new thing in their life.

5. Chased. To dream of being chased is symbolic of being pursued by a spiritual or physical enemy, Deut. 1:44. If you are being chased by authority figures like police officers, school principals or other adults, it may symbolize a problem with submitting yourself to authority.

6. Teeth. To dream of teeth that are cracked, loose or falling out may be an expression of suppressed anxieties over aging. The fear of getting older, a fast-paced lifestyle or depression in someone's life can be the culprit of these dreams. In a God-given dream teeth can also symbolize a person's words, Ps. 57:4.

7. Violence. Being shot, stabbed, raped or murdered during a dream is a reflection of demonic activity in a person's life or watching violent movies and video games, Lk.11:34.

8. Sex. A sexually explicit dream can result from being in an intimate relationship with someone or an expressed sexual desire. Sexual content is frequently the result of an influence from a demonic spirit of perversion.

A.

Abandoned car-symbolic of an unused ministry or a forsaken lifestyle, Ezek. 34:8 NLT

Abandoned house-symbolic of barrenness and desolation, Job 15:28

Abandoned road-symbolic of following your own plans or stubbornness, Jer. 18:15

Aborigine-symbolic of solitude

Abortion-an abortion may symbolize the premature death of a new thing in your life or the actual act of aborting an unborn child

Acid-a symbol of destructive words that burn long after they have been spoken, Prov. 16:27 NLT

Actor-an actor can symbolize playing a role, Ezek. 5:2 NLT. To see an actor in a dream may also be the result of a desire to interact with celebrities

Adders-spiritual enemies, Jer. 8:17

Admiral-symbolic of high command

Adoption-symbolic of caring for orphans or being welcomed into God's family, Rom. 8:15

Adulteress-symbolic of the path of death and destruction, Prov. 2:16

Adultery-sexually explicit dream content is not from God. To dream of an adulterous relationship may result from fear of infidelity in a relationship. A God-given dream may expose a cheating spouse without showing lewd conduct, Ex. 20:14

Aging-symbolic of wisdom and honor, Deut. 32:7

AIDS-symbolic of the need for compassion on outcasts and the terminally ill, Mark 1:40-42

Air-conditioning-symbolic of a luxury, modern comforts

Air force-symbolic of high level spiritual warfare or a prayer covering for other Christians

Aircraft carrier-symbolic of support during a spiritual battle or a base of operations

Airliner-an airliner can symbolize a world-wide ministry for a Christian or a fast-paced lifestyle for a non-believer

Airport-an airport symbolizes departure from one place in life to the next

Alarm-symbolic of being alerted or awakened to do something, Num. 10:5

Alcohol-if you dream of drinking alcohol it can symbolize a current or former addiction to alcohol, Prov. 20:1

Alcoholic-an emblem for the road to poverty, Prov. 23:20

Alien (space alien) symbolic of heavenly visitors. Aliens can be either demons or angels depending on the context of the dream

Alligator-a dangerous person or a spiritual enemy

Almonds-delicacies, Gen 43:11

Almond blossoms-symbolic of God's anointing upon a ministry, Num. 17:8

Almond tree-an almond tree is a symbol of God's promise to perform His word, Jer. 1:11

Aloe-a symbol of Christ's death, Jn. 19:39

Altar-a symbol of sacrifice, Ex. 20:24

Ambulance-symbolic of needing immediate help

Ambush-a symbol of an impending attack from an enemy, Prov. 1:11

Amish-symbolic of trying not to conform to the world around you

Amplifier-symbolic of a loud message

Amusement park-fun and entertainment, enjoyment in life

Anaconda-symbolic of a crushing problem like depression or anxiety in someone's life. Snakes represent demonic spirits, Isa. 59:4-5

Anarchy-symbolic of rebellion, 1 Sam. 15:23

Anchor-symbolic of hope, Heb. 6:19

Angels-symbolic of God's helpers and protection, Heb. 1:14

Angry-an angry person in a dream is symbolic of foolishness and pride, Prov. 12:16

Animals-talking animals can be demonic spirits posing as spirit guides. Running on all fours in a dream like an animal may represent a subconscious feeling of being powerful

Answering machine-symbolic of collecting messages you need to hear

Antarctica-symbolic of isolation and remoteness

Anteater-symbolic of something that destroys what others have worked hard to build

Antenna-symbolic of needing to pay close attention or tune in to God

Antiques-symbolic of sentimental possessions

Ants-symbolic of industriousness or tiny nuisances, Prov. 6:6. Ant bites symbolize misfortune, Deut. 32:23-24

Ape-a symbol of an overly emotional or beastly person

Apocalypse-a symbol of the end-times, Rev. 13:7

Apple-symbolic of forbidden fruit or something desirable to the eyes, Gen. 3:6. A golden apple is symbolic of wise words, Prov. 25. 11. Apples can also symbolize a time of refreshing, Song. 2:5

Apple tree-a symbol of the love of a husband, Song. 2:3

Apprentice-symbolic of learning to specialize in a field of work, 1 Kings 19:19-21

Apricot-sharing love and affection with a romantic partner

April fool's day-symbolic of an impending prank or trick

Apron-serving others, 1 Sam. 18:4

Aquarium-symbolic of being trapped or feeling examined

AR-15 (see Guns)

Arab-symbolic of the Middle East and Islam

Archaeologist-symbolic of digging into a matter or hunting for hidden knowledge

Architect-symbolic of heavenly wisdom, Prov. 8:30

Ark-God's protection from life's storms, Gen. 7:1

Ark of the Covenant-symbolic of God's power, Ex. 25:10

Arm-a right arm is a symbol of God's strength and might, Ps. 89:13, Isa. 62:8

Armadillo-symbolic of being well protected

Armageddon-symbolic of an end-times event, Rev. 16:16

Armband-a symbol of allegiance. The insignia on the band can give insight into the interpretation, Song. 8:6

Armor-armor is symbolic of God's provision of protection for Christians, Eph. 6:11

Armory-a symbol of bringing stored weapons to bear against an enemy, Jer. 50:25

Army-symbolic of a group of people with the same goals united for a cause, Phil. 2:25

Aroma-a foul aroma is symbolic of a spiritually dead person. A sweet aroma is symbolic of a Christian, 2 Cor. 2:16

Arrow-lies and deceit, Jer. 9:8. A poison arrow is symbolic of grief, Job 6:2-4

Art-symbolic of the beauty and wisdom of man, Acts 17:29

Artillery-to dream of field artillery can symbolize a battle in your life or a need to bring out bigger weapons to win a fight

Artist-skill, beauty, Song. 7:1

Ash-complete destruction, Amos 2:1

Ashen-an ashen figure symbolizes death, Rev. 6:8

Asia-symbolic of Eastern philosophy and religious influences, Acts 19:27

Aspirin-symbolic of help and relief from pain

Assassins-symbolic of demonic forces with a special mission to kill, steal and destroy, Jn. 10:10

Assault rifle (see Guns)

Assembly hall-symbolic of a gathering of people who are similar to each other in lifestyle or beliefs, James 2:2, Jer. 9:2

Asteroid-potential destruction, Rev. 8:10 NLT

Astrological sign-symbolic of pagan customs and influences, Jer. 10:2-3

Astronaut-symbolic of visiting heavenly places or seeing other worldly things

Atheist-symbolic of a person who is unwise and without understanding, Ps. 53:1

Athlete-competing in life, 1 Cor. 9:26

ATM-symbolic of trying to pull money from God or other people

Attic-symbolic of your mind, forgotten memoires or the subconscious

Attorney-someone skilled in debate, Lk.10:25

Auditorium-symbolic of a place where similar people are gathered. To find yourself in an auditorium with dead people or zombies is symbolic of having wandered away from the truth, Prov. 21:16-17

Autumn-time to work, Prov. 20:4

Avatar-symbolic of being controlled by someone or attempting to use other people

Axe-a battle axe is the word of God, Ezek. 9:2. If the axe head is dull it symbolizes the need to use the wisdom of God in a situation, Eccl. 10:10

B.

Baboon-symbolic of acting poorly in social settings

Baby-babies can symbolize a new thing being brought into a person's life, Isa. 42:9. A baby is also symbolic of a gift from God, Ps. 127:3

Baby carriage-symbolic of expecting a child or a new thing in life

Back (body part) if a person turns their back on you in a dream this symbolizes an attempt to ignore or dismiss you, Jer. 32:33

Backhoe-symbolic of a major renovation or a time of building yourself up in life

Backpack-symbolic of being a student or carrying too many things around with you

Backsliding-relapsing into old behavior, Hosea 4:16

Backstage-symbolic of helping behind the scenes

Bacteria-symbolic of the cause or root of trouble

Bad breath-to dream of having bad breath can symbolize a poor choice of words during a conversation or being self-conscious

Badge-symbolic of authority

Badger (animal) symbolic of pestering or bothering someone

Bag-symbolic of a journey, Isa. 10:28. The contents of the bag will give you more insight into the interpretation of the symbol

Baggage-symbolic of the things people drag with them from previous relationships. Baggage is also symbolic of God forcing someone to move, Ezek. 12:6

Bagpipes-to dream of a windbag instrument can symbolize speech that has no value or a speaker without any credibility, Jer. 5:13

Bait-symbolic of a lure or trap, Amos 3:5

Bakery-symbolic of producing spiritual sustenance for others or being in the service of another, Gen. 40:1

Balance-attempting to balance yourself in a dream is symbolic of a stressful event in life or trying to keep yourself emotionally stable during turbulent times, Ps. 119:109 NLT

Bald-losing your hair in a dream may symbolize not having protection from God, Micah 1:16

Ball-symbolic of a person's sphere of influence, 1 Cor. 10:13

Ballroom-having fun in life

Balm-a symbol of healing for a sick or wounded person, Jer. 8:22

Banana-symbolic of a delicacy or good spiritual fruit in your life

Banana republic-symbolic of the countries of Guatemala and Honduras (a call to prayer)

Band-symbolic of collaboration and teamwork, Ps. 68:25

Band aid-symbolic of trying to help a large problem with very few resources

Bandage-symbolic of healing and recovery, Isa. 1:6

Bandits-symbolic of a group of demons sent to raid someone, Hosea 7:1

Bank-symbolic of investment and security, Lk.19:23

Banner-symbolic of victory in Christ, Ps. 20:5 and God's love, Song. 2:4

Banquet-a banqueting hall or table set with food is symbolic of fellowship with Christ, Song. 2:4. Sitting at a dark table is symbolic of ungodly activities in your life, 1 Cor. 10:21

Baptism-symbolic of becoming fully immersed or initiated into something, Matt. 28:16-20. Watching someone attempt to baptize themselves is symbolic of trying to work for or earn salvation

Bar-symbolic of a bad environment or being surrounded by sinful people and spiritual enemies, 1 Cor. 6:10

Barbarian-symbolic of a person that you cannot understand, 1 Cor. 14:11

Barbecue-roasting food can be symbolic of feeling satisfied for a period of time in life, Isa. 44:16

Barbed wire-to dream of barbed wire suggests a hindrance to your movement in life

Barking-symbolic of a warning, Isa. 56:10. Barking may also be a spiritual enemy attempting to intimidate you

Barn-symbolic of a person's stored wealth, Prov. 3:9. A barn can also symbolize a person's life and property, Ps. 144:13, Jer. 50:26

Barricade-protection, Song. 8:9

Baseball-symbolic of competing in the game of life

Basket-symbolic of carrying a burden, Ps. 81:6. A basket can be symbolic of blessing and prosperity if you are carrying good fruit

Basketball-symbolic of the game of life. If the defenders are taller than you it symbolizes a spiritual struggle. If you are playing well it symbolizes a good season in your life

Bat (bat-like creature) symbolic of a demonic entity, an unclean animal, Lev. 11:19

Bathing-symbolic of cleansing yourself, Ex. 30:19-21. Bathing is also symbolic of a place of intimacy and exposure, 2 Sam. 11:2

Bathroom-symbolic of exposure or an invasion of privacy. If the bathroom is filthy it may be an indication of a dirty lifestyle, 2 Sam. 11:2

Batman-to dream of being Batman can symbolize fighting against spiritual forces of wickedness, 2 Cor. 10:4-5

Battering ram-to dream of a battering ram or siege engine is symbolic of being engaged in a spiritual battle, Deut. 20:20

Battle-symbolic of the struggle to live a virtuous life in accordance with God's word, Ps. 78:9-10

Battleship-symbolic of heavy spiritual bombardment

Bazooka-symbolic of blasting your enemies with destructive words

Beach-if you are on a beach looking out at the water it symbolizes waiting for something in life. If you are walking or sunning yourself on a beach it symbolizes tranquility. A beach can also symbolize waiting for the return of Christ, Isa. 42:4

Bear-symbolic of ferocity, 2 Kings 2:24

Beast-symbolic of an enemy or an arrogant person, Eccl. 3:18. Running on all fours like a beast in a dream may be symbolic of being powerful

Beaten-if you are being beaten in dream it can be emblematic of a demonic attack. If you are being beaten on the back with a rod it can symbolize correction for foolish behavior, Prov. 10:13

Beaver-industrious, hard-working

Bed-a place of intimacy, Heb. 13:4, rest or privacy, 2 Kings 6:12. If a person is sick in bed it can symbolize a sinful lifestyle, Ezek. 23:17. A fragrant, clean bed is symbolic of righteous living, Prov. 7:17

Bedroom-symbolic of a private area, 2 Kings 6:12

Bee-a swarm of bees can be a symbol of acting presumptuously against an overwhelming enemy, Ps. 118:12, Deut. 1:44

Beer-symbolic of brawling, Prov. 20:1

Beetles-a hard to kill problem

Begging-symbolic of a curse, Ps. 109:10

Belching-wicked words, Ps. 59:7

Bell-a call to attention or warning, Ex. 28:33-35. Golden bells are symbolic of ministry and holiness, Ex. 28:34

Belt-this is symbolic of truth, Eph. 6:11. A belt is also symbolic of an attachment to something, Jer. 13:11

Bestiality-a spirit of perversion, Lev. 18:23

Bible-to dream of the Bible is symbolic of the need to read God's word, 2 Tim. 3:16

Bicycle-symbolic of a person's movement through life. If the bike has broken parts or missing wheels it symbolizes problems or troubles with the person riding the bike

Bigfoot-symbolic of a large problem in your life like depression or anger

Billboard-a sign or warning marker, something you need to see and pay attention to in a dream, Isa. 8:1

Binoculars-symbolic of seeing beyond your present situation

Biohazard-to see a biohazard sign in a dream is a warning of deadly things in your life

Bird-a messenger, Eccl. 10:20

Birth-symbolic of a new thing in your life, Isa. 42:9

Birthday Cake-celebratory of a person's life and growth. If the cake is half-baked or burnt it symbolizes worthlessness Hosea 7:8

Bishop (see Chess)

Biting-dreaming of being bitten or biting others is symbolic of strife and quarreling, Gal. 5:15

Bitterness-symbolic of the results of sin, Prov. 5:3

Black belt-an expert in spiritual warfare

Black cat-a black cat can symbolize evil or bad luck for many non-Christians and is a common dream symbol in many nightmares

Black horse-symbolic of famine, Rev. 6:5

Black sheep-an outcast or misfit

Black widow spider-a demonic spirit, Isa. 59:4-5

Blanket-symbolic of a love for others or covering mistakes, Acts 9:36

Blast furnace-a hard life, worldly living, a person's life before Christ, Jer. 11:4

Bleach-complete cleansing

Blemish-sin or perceived flaws, Song. 4:7

Blind-being without godly instruction, Prov. 29:18. Being blind can also symbolize the need for brotherly love in your life, 2 Pet. 1:9

Blindfold-a spiritual blockage to a person's ability to see the truth, 2 Cor. 4:4

Blizzard-this is symbolic of blindness in a situation or resistance in life

Blood-a symbol of the sacrifice of Christ on the cross, Matt. 26:28. Washing in blood is a symbol of exacting vengeance, Ps. 58:10

Bloody-a person covered in blood is emblematic of killing and death, Hosea 6:8

Bloody water-emblematic of war, trouble and woe, Isa. 15:9

Bluebird-order, obedience, Jer. 8:7

Bluffing-symbolic of not thinking something through, Prov. 21:29

Blushing-symbolic of embarrassment or shame, Jer. 6:15

Boa constrictor-depression or anxiety, a demonic attacker, Isa. 59:4-5

Boar-devourer, a symbol of a curse upon your valuables or property, Ps. 80:13

Boat-symbolic of a vehicle for ministry or the way someone lives their life

Body-a direct reference to the flesh. An emaciated body symbolizes sin in a person's life, Ps. 31:10

Body armor-this is symbolic of a well-protected Christian, Eph. 6:13

Bodybuilder-a wise man, Prov. 24:5. Also symbolic of moral and physical strength, Amos 2:14. Bodybuilders may also imply people who intimidate you

Bodyguard-a close spiritual advisor, a friend and protector, 1 Sam. 22:14

Bogyman-a demonic oppressor

Boiling water-a symbol of evil being poured out on people, Jer. 1:14

Boils-symbolic of evil in a person's life. If the boil is on their lips it means they speak with unkind words

Bomb-symbolic of something that will cause major problems or damage

Bomber (airplane) symbolic of spiritual warfare or end-times events

Bones-symbolic of spiritual death and hopelessness, Ezek. 37:11. A broken bone can symbolize a wound inflicted by God, Ps. 51:8

Book-the meaning of a book can be ascertained by its title or the words written in the pages. If you are surrounded by books it can be symbolic of a love of reading and knowledge

Book-of-life-to dream of the book-of-life is symbolic of God's salvation or an invitation to accept Christ as lord and savior, Ps. 69:28

Boomerang-something that will come right back to you

Boot-symbolic of war, Isa. 8:5. Boots can also symbolize being prepared to give the gospel, Eph. 6:15

Boot camp-symbolic of preparation and training

Boss-symbolic of authority. A boss may symbolize a parent, teacher, guardian or supervisor

Bottle-symbolic of the need to keep information secret

Bow and arrow-the weapons of God against an enemy, Ps 21:1. If the bow is bent it means you are ready for battle, Isa. 5:28

Bowing-symbolic of submission, being burdened with work or the cares of life, Ps. 145:14. If you are bowing down in a dream if symbolizes that you serve that person or object, Mal. 1:6

Boxer-fighting, hostility, 1 Cor. 9:26

Boy Scout-helping others, civically minded

Brakes-symbolic of needing to slow down or stop doing something

Branch-symbolic of Christ, Zech. 3:8

Branded-branding can symbolize having something permanently etched in your mind. Branding can mean that your mind is closed off, 1 Tim. 4:2

Branding iron-symbolic of slavery, Isa. 3:24, 1 Tim. 4:2

Brazen face-symbolic of not having any fear, Prov. 7:13

Bread-this is symbolic of the broken body of Christ and the fellowship of friends, Matt. 26:26

Bread and butter-something that will bring you guaranteed income

Breastplate-symbolic of the righteousness of Christ, faith and love, Eph. 6:1, 1 Thess. 5:8

Breathing fire-symbolic of destructive words, Jer. 5:14

Bribe-wickedness, Isa. 1:23

Bricks-symbolic of slave labor and hard work, 2 Sam. 12:31

Bride-symbolic of the church, Rev. 21:9. To dream of a bride may also foretell marriage

Bridal gown-symbolic of being prepared for marriage

Bridal shower-symbolic of finding love or being celebrated

Bridegroom-symbolic of Christ, Matt. 9:15

Bridge-symbolic of crossing over to a new place in life

Bridle-a curse, stubbornness, Prov. 26:3

Briefcase-symbolic of professionalism and industry

Brimstone-the judgment of God against the wicked, Ps. 11:6

Broken arms-symbolic of being powerless, Ps. 37:17

Broken pot-this is a symbol of someone who has died or passed away because of grief in life or having been crushed by sin, Ps. 31:12

Broken window-this can symbolize having your peace or joy stolen by a spiritual thief, Joel 2:9

Bronze-symbolic of strength, Micah 4:13

Bronze gate-symbolic of imprisonment, Ps. 107:16

Bronze wall-symbolic of strength, Jer. 1:18

Brook-a bubbling stream is symbolic of wisdom, Prov. 18:4

Broom-symbolic of cleaning out your life, Isa. 14:23

Broomstick-a person flying on a broomstick is symbolic of witchcraft and spiritual enemies fighting against you

Brother-symbolic of Christ, Prov. 18:24, other Christians or adversity, Prov. 17:17

Brownies-symbolic of love, fellowship, food and family

Bruise-to dream of bruising is symbolic of wounds from life's trials, Job 9:17

Bubble gum-if you have gum on you it can symbolize a tricky situation. Blowing bubbles may symbolize immaturity

Buccaneer-a hard-living and argumentative person

Buck-symbolic of a lover, fiancé or husband, Song. 2:9

Bucket-if the bucket is flowing with water it symbolizes prosperity and life in the spirit, Num. 24:7

Buddha-to see Buddha in a dream is symbolic of a spirit of false religion

Buffet-life's choices

Bug bites-symbolic of misfortune, Deut. 32:23-24

Builder-a person building something is symbolic of wisdom, Prov. 14:1

Buildings-buildings symbolize areas and places you frequent. Any place where people come together can manifest itself as a building in a dream

Bull-a bull is symbolic of a strong enemy, Ps. 22:12

Bulldog-tenacity

Bulldozer-clearing ground in life or tearing things down

Bullet-a symbol of a malicious word or the word of God aimed at a spiritual enemy, Ps. 10:7. A blank or empty cartridge is symbolic of ineffective prayer

Bulletproof vest-a symbol of protection against attack, a well-armed Christian, Eph. 6:11

Bullfrog-symbolic of a demon, Rev. 16:13-14

Bum-an outcast or wandering person can symbolize a spiritual oppressor or being cast-out from the presence of God, Gen. 4:12

Bumper sticker-symbolic of a position you endorse or message you propagate

Bunny-for many non-Christians a bunny symbolizes luck, fertility and magical power

Burden-this can be a symbol for a person's sins or anxieties in life, Ps. 38:4, Matt. 11:30. A burden can also symbolize other people's problems, Gal. 6:2

Bureaucrat-a difficult and inflexible person, Isa. 10:1

Burglar-a sign of demonic activity surrounding your house and family intent on stealing your peace, Jn. 10:10

Burglarized-to have your property stolen or broken into during a dream is symbolic of a spiritual thief, Prov. 23:28

Burning coals-cleansing, Isa. 6:6, or kindness, Prov. 25:22

Burping-symbolic of wicked talk, Ps. 59:7

Bus-this is symbolic of a large ministry for a Christian or the ride of life for a non-believer

Busboy-symbolic of serving others in a lowly fashion

Bush-this can symbolize a person's growth in life or a call to ministry from God, Ex. 3:4

Butler (cupbearer) symbolic of a trusted position of service, 1 Kings 10:5

Butter-symbolic of the blessing and friendship of God, Job 29:6

Butterfly-beauty or a socially adept person

Buzzard-a demon, Rev. 18:2 NLT

C.

Cabin-a log-cabin can be symbolic of the need for seclusion

Cactus-a cactus can symbolize a hindrance to your progress in life

Caddie-carrying someone else's workload or a trusted advisor

Cage-symbolic of being trapped, Jer. 5:26-27

Cake-celebratory of a person's life. If the cake is half-baked or burnt it symbolizes worthlessness, Hosea 7:8

Calculator-examining or calculating the cost of something, Lk.14:28

Calendar-the seasons of a person's life or waiting for a specific day or event to happen, Job 14:13 NLT

Calf (young cow) symbolic of a weak person or nation, Ps. 68:30

Camel-symbolic of something that is impossible to accomplish without God's help, Mark 10:25

Camera-symbolic of memories or capturing the moment. If someone is taking your picture the dream is drawing attention to your life

Camouflage-blending in or going unnoticed

Camping-symbolic of a temporary situation, Ex. 14:1

Candle-a person's life, Matt. 12:20

Candy-to dream about candy can be symbolic of a desire to eat sweets, Isa. 29:8. Candy can also symbolize a lure or temptation

Cannibalism-symbolic of gossip and slander, Gal. 5:15. Devouring people is also symbolic of injustice and oppression of the poor, Micah 3:1-3

Cannon-spiritual weaponry

Capital building-symbolic of rule, authority, government, Rom. 13:1

Captain-an official position of authority, Num. 31:48

Car-cars can be symbolic of a Christian ministry. If the person is not a Christian a car symbolizes the way a person lives their life. A car with body damage is indicative of a person who has a careless lifestyle

Caravan-symbolic of traveling with others for the same purpose and for safety, Gen. 37:25, Lk. 2:44

Cardinal-a symbol of importance or high rank

Caribbean-rest, relaxation

Carport-symbolic of a covering or the need to protect your life or ministry

Carried-if you are being carried in a dream it symbolizes protection, shepherding or covering by God or the person carrying you, Ps. 28:9

Cartel-an organized group of spiritual enemies

Cartoon-watching cartoons during a dream is symbolic of silliness or immature behavior for an adult

Casino-a casino is symbolic of worldly living. The games within are symbolic of gambling with your life. Winning at a casino is symbolic of the treasures of the world

Castle-symbolic of a stronghold, 2 Kings 15:25

Cat-to dream of your pet cat may symbolize worries and fears about your pet's wellbeing. A black cat may symbolize woe to an unbeliever

Catapult-being launched from a catapult can symbolize moving forward in life very quickly

Caterpillar-a devouring curse, Amos 4:9

Cathedral-symbolic of old religion

Catholicism-piety and religious ritual

Cattle prod-wise sayings, the word of God, Eccl. 12:11

Caution sign-symbolic of a warning, Jude 1:23 NLT

Cave-this can be a secret and difficult area to get to in life. A cave can also be symbolic of being trapped, Isa. 42:22

Caveman-symbolic of a rude, brutish person

Cedar tree-a strong, flourishing person, Ps. 92:12

Celebrity-to dream of a celebrity can symbolize the desire to interact with famous people or to become famous yourself

Cellphone-to dream of an incessantly ringing cellphone is symbolic of being busy or overly talkative

Cemetery-symbolic of being spiritually dead, Matt. 8:28 NLT

Certificate-to be given a certificate in a dream is symbolic of being granted authorization to do something, Neh. 10:1, Ester 8:8

Chaff-a symbol of a wicked and worthless person, Ps. 35:5

Chains-to dream of being chained is symbolic of sin, addiction or being bound by Satan, Eccl. 7:26

Chair-a large chair is symbolic of authority, Song. 3:9

Chameleon-symbolic of blending in or a person who likes frequent change

Champagne-symbolic of victory

Champion-a champion boxer or a championship belt symbolizes God's protection, Jer. 20:11

Chariot-a vehicle for war, Ps. 20:7

Chased-to dream of being chased is symbolic of being pursued by a spiritual or physical enemy, Deut. 1:44. If you are being chased by authority figures like police officers, school principals or other adults, it may symbolize a problem with submitting yourself to authority

Chasing the wind-stupidity, folly, worthless tasks, Eccl. 2:26

Cheating-to dream of cheating on a test or at a game can symbolize the use of underhanded tactics in your life, Gen. 31:7

Cheating (relationships) see Adultery

Check (paycheck) finding a check in a dream can symbolize receiving unexpected income. A check may also represent the wages of someone's life, Rom. 6:23

Checkmate-symbolic of assured victory in a situation

Cheerleader-to dream of being a cheerleader is symbolic of a positive, uplifting and supportive person

Cheetah-speed, agility

Chef-a master at serving others

Chess-symbolic of being locked in a strategic battle with people or spiritual enemies

Chicken-a symbol of fear or cowardice

Chief-symbolic of leadership, Prov. 6:7

Chihuahua-a Chihuahua can symbolize a yappy, gossiping person, Prov. 20:19 NLT

Children-symbolic of God's blessing, joy and peace, Zech. 8:5

Chimney-smoke from a chimney symbolizes something that will quickly disappear in life, Hose 13:3

China-symbolic of Chinese people or Eastern religious beliefs

Chisel-symbolic of something man-made or permanently etched into a person's heart, Isa. 44:13, Jer. 17:1

Chocolate-to dream of chocolate may symbolize an affinity for or desire to eat sweets, Isa. 29:8

Choking-if you are choking yourself in a dream it is an indication of a poor self-image. If you are choking someone else it can symbolize hatred for that person. If you are being choked in a dream the source can be the worries of the world and a pursuit of wealth, Matt. 13:22. If you are watching someone get strangled it can be a warning about a physical or spiritual attack on that person

Christmas tree-family, holidays, thankfulness

Church-to dream of a church can symbolize a person's religious activities or beliefs about Christianity, Heb. 12:23

Cigarette-symbolic of an addictive and negative behavior

Cinderella-symbolic of feeling used or disrespected by others

Cinnamon-symbolic of a holy anointing, something pleasing and set apart for God, Ex. 30:23-25

Circles-a symbol of unity, eternity, something unending. Walking in circles during a dream is symbolic of wandering in a spiritual wilderness, Deut. 2:3

Circus-dreaming of being at the circus is symbolic of a bustling atmosphere

City-symbolic of a busy and bustling life. If the city is filled with happy people it symbolizes righteousness. If the city is on a high hill it symbolizes blessing. If the city is being torn down or in ruins it symbolizes wickedness, Prov. 11:10-11

City (dark) symbolizes Satan's influence over a person or an area in which they live, Ps. 74:20

City (golden) symbolic of Zion the city of God, Rev. 21:2

Civil war-arguing with friends or family, 1 Cor. 1:10

Clapping-a sign of the joy of the Lord, Ps. 47:1. Clapping is also symbolic of approval

Clay-symbolic of a Christian, Isa. 64:8, or the human body, Job 4:19

Climbing-moving up in life or on the job, trying to get a better position in life

Cloak-symbolic of something hidden or mysterious, Judg. 3:16

Clock- symbolic of waiting, an issue that is dependent upon God's timing, 2 Pet. 3:9

Closet-symbolic of private prayer, Matt. 6:6. A closet may also symbolize a place where people bury things from their life that they do not wish to deal with

Clothes-if the clothes are white it symbolizes the righteousness of Christ, Rev. 3:5. If the clothes are spotted or soiled it symbolizes sin in a person's life, Rev. 3:4. Dirty clothes symbolize dead works, Isa. 64:6

Clouds-if the cloud is dark and foreboding it symbolizes trouble or a storm in life. If the cloud is white it symbolizes God's majesty and peace. If it is a rain cloud it can symbolize God's favor, Prov. 16:15. Dreaming of a rain cloud that does not deliver rain when expected is symbolic of bragging about abilities and gifts that someone does not possess, Prov. 25:14

Clown-a clown can symbolize happiness and joy. If seen in a nightmare a clown can represent a demonic heckler

Club-an instrument of war symbolic of God's words shattering His enemies, Jer. 51:20

Coal-a cleansing agent from God's altar, Isa. 6:6. Coals are also symbolic of kindness, Prov. 25:22

Coast (sea coast) symbolic of waiting for Christ, Isa, 42:4

Coat-a valuable possession symbolic of generosity towards others, James 2:15-16

Coattail-attaching yourself to another person's success

Cobra-a wicked person or demon, Ps. 58:4

Cocaine (see Drugs)

Cockroach-symbolic of living in a dirty environment

Coffin-a coffin is symbolic of a person dying physically, mentally and emotionally. A coffin can symbolize someone coming out of spiritual death into life in Christ, Eph. 2:5

Cog-symbolic of being a small but crucial part of an organization, 1 Cor. 12:29

Coin-symbolic of stewardship, Matt. 25:14

Cold drink-refreshing, good news, Prov. 25:25

Collage-symbolic of higher learning, Acts 19:9

Coma-a coma is symbolic of having your true personality put aside or being out of touch with reality in life, a feeling of detachment

Comet-a comet can be symbolic of destruction and end-times events, Rev. 8:10 NLT

Compass-symbolic of finding the right direction in life, Ps. 119:59 NLT

Complaining-to dream of someone complaining is symbolic of a rebellious person, Job 23:2

Computer-gathering or disseminating information

Concentration camp-this is symbolic of a spiritual prison or a place that is oppressive

Convertible-a fancy ministry or ease in life

Conveyor belt-a symbol of being taken in a direction outside of your will and control

Convict-symbolic of spiritual enemies, 2 Pet. 2:4

Cop-law enforcement officials represent earthly or spiritual authority, 1 Pet. 2:13

Coral-beauty, high value, Job 28:18

Corner-to come upon a corner in dream is symbolic of an unexpected circumstance in life that will cause you to change direction suddenly

Corner of the house-symbolic of living with an argumentative person, Prov. 21:9

Corpse-to see a corpse in a dream is symbolic of spiritual death and judgment, Ps. 110:6

Costume-playing a role or pretending to be someone you are not

Couch-symbolic of relaxing. If you see a couch that is colorful it can symbolize an adulterous woman, Prov. 7:16

Counsel-symbolic of the path to victory, Prov. 11:14

Counselor-Jesus, the Holy Spirit, Isa. 9:6

Counterfeit money-false teaching, 2 Pet. 2:1

Court-being held accountable for your actions or judging the actions of others, Matt. 5:22

Covering-symbolic of loving others, Prov. 10:12

Cow-oppressive, wealthy women who live in leisurely ease, Amos 4:1

Cowboy-this is symbolic of a loner, someone who is self-sufficient

Crane (bird) symbolic of mindless chatter, Isa. 38:14

Crane (machine) symbolic of a major project or season of building-up in someone's life

Craps (dice game) symbolic of taking chances or a gamble in a situation

Crazy person (see mental patient)

Creditor-if you dream of a creditor it can symbolize a curse on someone's life, Ps. 109:11

Crocodile-symbolic of something harmful, an old, lurking, spiritual enemy

Crooked mouth-a symbol of perverse or wicked speech, Prov. 8:8

Cross-symbolic of Christ's death for our sins, Jn. 19:19. If the cross is colored the color has special significance to the interpretation. A cross can be on an animal or a person and be an indication of a false religious belief or demonic doctrine

Cross-dresser-to see a man wearing women's clothes or a woman wearing men's clothing during a dream is symbolic of someone who is oppressed and influenced by a demonic spirit of perversion, Deut. 22:5

Crossroads-decisions or choices in life, Jer. 6:16 NLT

Crow-mockery

Crowd-a crowd can symbolize the masses or people around the world. A crowd can also symbolize a compromise of your values, Ex. 23:2 NLT

Crown-symbolic of royalty and power, Rev. 14:14

Cruise ship-to dream of being aboard a cruise liner is symbolic of an easy position in life. If the ship is sinking it symbolizes disaster or troubles in life

Crushed-symbolic of being overwhelmed by a situation or a person. Feeling crushed can also be symbolic of sin in a person's life, Ps. 38:8

Crying-needing help, grieving, Prov. 21:13

Crystal-value and worth, Job 28:18

Crystal ball-symbolic of divination and witchcraft, Zech. 10:2, Acts 16:16 NLT

Crystal methamphetamines (see Drugs)

Cub (animal) to dream of baby animals may symbolize playfulness or caring. A bear cub can be symbolic of fierce anger, 2 Sam. 17:8

Cup-to dream of sharing a cup with someone symbolizes shared beliefs or activities, 1 Cor. 10:21. A cup can also symbolize being used by God, Jer. 51:7

Cursing-symbolic of worthlessness and wickedness, Prov. 6:11

Curtain-symbolic of concealment, Matt. 27:51, Heb. 6:1

Custodian-symbolic of an official position of trust, one who takes care of a facility, 1 Chron. 9:17-26

Cypress tree-symbolic of God, Hosea 14:8

D.

Dam-building a dam is symbolic of trying to uncover hidden, earthly treasures, Job 28:10-12

Dancing-symbolizes God's grace and help in a time of trouble, Ps. 30:10-11. If people are dancing at a night club it can be symbolic of a wild lifestyle, 1 Pet. 4:3 NLT

Dark path-an evil place or the way of the wicked, Ps.35:6

Darkness-symbolic of being surrounded by evil or in need of God's light, Joel 2:2

Dart (see poison arrow)

Darts (game) symbolic of being on target or aiming at something particular

Date (fruit) symbolic of beauty and love, Song. 5:11

Date (romantic) symbolic of a love interest in your life

Daughter-uniqueness, Song. 6:9

Dawn-loving-kindness, Ps. 92:2

Deacon-honor, dignity, trustworthiness, 1 Tim. 3:8

Dead body-to see a dead body in a dream can be symbolic of spiritual death or someone who has been attacked by Satan, Ps. 110:6

Deadwood-symbolic of spiritual death, Jude 1:12

Death-to dream of someone dying may be a warning of impending physical death. Death may also symbolize a person's need for a spiritual awakening, Eph. 2:5. Dreaming of death may also be caused by demonic influences

Death row-inescapable punishment

Debt collector-symbolic of a curse upon someone's life, Ps. 109:11

Debtor-someone who does not repay debts is symbolic of foolish behavior, Ps. 37:21, Lk.14:28-29

Decoy-lure, bait, trap, 2 Cor. 2:11 NLT

Deep water-symbolic of a spiritual river, Ezek. 47:5

Deer-a symbol of peace and longing, Ps. 42:1. Deer are also symbolic of youth and beauty, Song. 4:5

Deer blind-symbolic of lying in wait for someone or something

Defensive fortification-this symbolizes God's protection over your life, Ps. 28:8

Demon-symbolic of evil spirits, 1 Cor. 10:21

Dentist-symbolic of the need to work on your choice of words, Prov. 16:24, 27 NLT

Deodorant-symbolic of covering up offensiveness

Department store-symbolic of life's choices

Depression-symbolic of being oppressed in life, Isa. 61:3

Desert-symbolic of a cursed or spiritually dry area, Jer. 51:43. The desert can also symbolize a place of insolation for a season in someone's life

Desk-a symbol of authority or an official office within the church, 1 Cor. 12:28. If the desk is a student's desk it symbolizes a time of learning

Despair-a feeling of despair in a dream is symbolic of lost hope and a need for God, Ps. 42:6

Detective-to dream of being a detective symbolizes that you are searching out the meaning of a matter in your life, Deut. 19:18

Devil-dreaming of the devil is symbolic of demonic activity and evil within your life or coming under attack, James 4:7

Dew-the dew on the grass is symbolic of God's favor, Prov. 19:12, Job 29:19

Diamond-symbolic of something of great worth, Ex. 28:18

Diamond back-a rattlesnake is a demon, Isa. 59:4-5

Diaper-a dirty diaper can be symbolic of filth or sin, Zeph. 1:17

Dieting-symbolic of being self-conscious or the desire to lose weight

Dice-throwing dice is symbolic of taking a risk in life

Dictator-symbolic of a domineering person. A dictator can be symbolic of your boss or spouse

Digging-symbolic of hard work, Lk.16:3, Deut. 8:9

Dinosaur-Dinosaur bones symbolize things in your life that have been planted and forgotten that will be valuable when uncovered at a later time

Diploma-authorization, mastery of a subject

Directions-to dream of a geographical direction can signal a location of interest for prayer. A direction can also be an answer from God concerning a move in life

Dirty clothes-symbolic of sin and dead works, Isa. 64:6

Disciple-symbolic of following Christ, Isa. 50:4

Discipline-to dream of someone willingly accepting discipline or correction symbolizes wisdom. To dream of someone fighting against or talking back to authority symbolizes stupidity, Prov. 12:1

Disease-symbolic of sin and curses, Deut. 7:15

Dishes-a dirty dish can symbolize hypocrisy and sin, Matt. 23:25. Clean dishes signify good and proper living

Disqualified-symbolic of a person who does not follow the rules, 1 Cor. 9:27

DJ (disc jockey) symbolic of being the source of other people's good time

Doctor-to dream of a medical doctor can be symbolic of Christ or a pastor. If you are the doctor in the dream it symbolizes your authority or expertise in a situation in life, Jer. 8:22

Doe-a young wife, Prov. 5:19

Dog-seeing a dog in a dream can symbolize ungrateful, worldly people or evil men, Ps 22:16, Matt. 7:6. Growling dogs can be demonic sentries sent to guard things. Your pet dog may appear in a dream because you are worried about the health of your pet. Dogs may also be representative of fears about being bitten or attacked by dogs

Dog ear-to dream of pulling a dog's ear is symbolic of meddling in other people's business, Prov. 26:17

Dogfight-symbolic of a fierce fight

Dominos-watching dominos fall can be symbolic of being the cause of a series of events

Donkey-a stubborn, mulish person, Job 11:12

Door-this is symbolic of an opening to a new path in life. If the door is locked it symbolizes an area in life not yet accessible to you. A person or animal blocking a door is symbolic of a spiritual hindrance. A door can also be symbolic of a free spirited person, Song. 8:8-9. Doors can also symbolize a person's mouth, Ps. 141:3

Doorway-a person waiting at an open door can symbolize the pursuit of wisdom, Prov. 8:34

Doppelgänger-a ghostly double of yourself is a demonic force that has assumed your image within a dream in order to frighten you. Many non-Christians who practice lucid dreaming report meeting their doppelgänger in a dream

Double edged sword-symbolic of the word of God, Heb. 4:12

Dove-symbolic of peace, rest and the Holy Spirit, Ps. 55:6. A dove may also be symbolic of a young woman, Song. 2:14

Downward spiral-symbolic of the path to death or moving in the wrong direction in life

Drag race-a person who lives an out-of-control, fast-paced lifestyle

Dragon-Satan, the devil, Rev. 12:9

Drain-symbolic of discarding something worthless

Dripping faucet (tub or sink) symbolic of disagreements and arguments, Prov.19:13

Driving-a fast driver is a person who is in a hurry in life. If the driver is reckless it symbolizes carelessness in life

Dross-wicked people, Prov. 25:4

Drowning-symbolic of an attack from people or the devil, Ps. 124:2-5

Drugs-a common theme in dreams is the use of illegal drugs. Dreaming about drug use can be an effect of having a current or former drug addiction

Dry ground-parched land is symbolic of ruin or apathy to spiritual things, Jer. 4:3, 48:18

Duck-a noisy or boisterous person

Dumpster-symbolizes something that needs to be removed from your life. If you are in a dumpster it can symbolize a worthless lifestyle, Phil. 3:8 NLT

Dung-symbolic of something worthless and discarded, Jer. 25:33

Dungeon-being in a dungeon symbolizes being a prisoner, Isa. 42:7

Dunk-to dream of dunking a ball in a game is symbolic of power and skill

Dust-symbolizes man and mortality, Gen. 2:7. Dust can also be symbolic of death, Ps. 30:9

Dust devil-symbolic of small or manageable troubles

Dying-symbolic of spiritual or physical death

Dynamite-symbolic of an explosive situation

E.

Eagle-symbolic of swiftness, 2 Sam. 1:23. An eagle can also be symbolic of an evil spirit depending on the context of the dream, Hosea 8:1

Ear-symbolic of needing to listen. Pulling an ear is symbolic of meddling in other people's business, Prov. 26:17

Earmuffs-symbolic of not wanting to hear something, Zech. 7:11

Earring-a golden earring is symbolic of wisdom or reproof, Prov. 25:12

Earthquake-symbolic of trouble and judgment, Nah. 1:5

East (see directions)

East-wind-symbolic of the knowledge of man or useless talk, Job 15:3

Easy-chair-a position of authority over a family or power within an organization, Song. 3:9

Eavesdropping-being a busybody, Prov. 17:9, 20:19

Eclipse-symbolic of end-times events, Joel 2:31

Ecstasy (see Drugs)

Edge-being on the edge of a building or cliff symbolizes a dangerous situation in which you need God's help and peace, Lk.4:29 NLT

Egg-an egg is a symbol of incubating wealth. Acquired unjustly the egg will be taken from you in the dream, Jer. 17:11 NLT

Egg white-symbolic of something tasteless and repulsive, Job 6:6

Egypt-symbolic of worldly living and a person's life before Christ, Heb. 3:16, Jude 1:5

Elderly-to see an elderly person is symbolic of wisdom and understanding, Ps. 119:100

Electricity-electric lights emanating from people or machines can symbolize high-tech weaponry or a person who is indwelt by the Holy Spirit, Matt. 28:3

Elementary school-symbolic of learning the basics, Gal. 4:1-3

Elephant-a large, obvious problem in someone's life

Elevated-if you are in an elevated position in a dream it symbolizes high social status or favor in life, Ps. 62:4

Elevator-to dream of being in an elevator is symbolic of ascending into a higher spiritual realm or a new place in life. To see an elevator in your dream is showing you a way up or out of your current surroundings

Elves-demonic spirits

Empty house-a symbol of feeling abandoned or alone in life, Isa. 27:10 NLT

End of the World-to dream of the end of the world is symbolic of a call to preparedness and repentance, Acts 2:17-21

Engine-symbolic of something critical to a person's health or success

Entangled-trouble, distress, bondage, Nah. 1:9-10

Eraser-symbolic of expunging mistakes, Ps. 34:16 NLT

Eunuch-symbolic of someone who is able to dedicate themselves to a cause, Matt. 19:12

Evangelism-symbolic of a wise person, Prov. 11:30

Ex-Lover-to dream of someone you had a relationship with symbolizes a tumultuous emotional experience (love or hate) with that person, Eph. 5:31, 1 Cor. 6:16

Exam-taking an exam is symbolic of being tested in life, James 1:3

Executioner-symbolic of someone who is tasked with carrying out unpleasant orders from other people, Dan. 2:14

Exile-punishment designed to purge you of wicked behavior in lieu of death, Jer. 29:1-16

Exit sign-a way out of trouble, 1 Cor. 10:13

Exorcism-symbolic of spiritual warfare in the authority of Christ, Mark 3:14-15

Exterminator-symbolic of someone who helps take care of problems in your life or the lives of others

Extra innings-symbolic of high pressure and intense competition during an event in life

Eye-symbolic of watching, seeing or knowing, Prov. 15:3. Large eyes are symbolic of seeing everything

Eye shadow-symbolic of arousal and sexuality, Jer. 4:30

Eyewash-symbolic of being a hypocrite, Matt. 7:5

F.

Faces-faces are symbolic of humanity. If the face is pale it symbolizes death or anguish, Joel 2:6. A gleaming, smiling face symbolizes joy and peace. A face without eyes, ears or mouth is symbolic of being deaf and dumb to the gospel, Ezek. 12:2

Factory-symbolic of work, school or a feeling of monotony in life. A factory symbolizes any place that is routine

Fair-symbolic of a fun place

Fairy-a familiar spirit

Faithfulness-symbolic of God's character and the fruit of the Spirit, Gal. 5:22

Fall (season) symbolic of change or a new thing in life

Falling-symbolic of a loss of control or uncontrollable circumstances in life. Watching someone else fall may be a warning for you to pray for the person in free-fall. Falling is also a sign of not having any godly guidance, Prov. 11:14

Family-to dream of your family members can be an attempt to draw attention to your relationship with them, Jer. 12:6 NLT. If a dream contains relatives who are deceased it can be showing you a generational curse or blessing that originates with that particular relative. If the dead relative is dripping with oil, radiant and joyous it symbolizes eternal life, 1 Jn. 3:9 NLT

Famine-misfortune, Deut. 32:23

Fangs-lies, wickedness, Ps. 58:6

Farming-symbolic of wisdom and plenty, Prov. 12:11

Fat-if you are eating fat in a dream it may indicate that you are taking things that belong to God, Lev. 3:16

Fat cat-symbolic of a rich person

Fate-symbolic of vanity and death, Eccl. 9:1-3

Fatigues-symbolic of the Lord's army, a Christian soldier, 2 Tim. 2:3

Fawn-youth, beauty, Song. 4:5

Fear-a dream where the overarching emotion is fear can be caused by anxieties in life, drug use or demonic activity, 2 Tim. 1:7

Feast-symbolic of happiness, fun, enjoyment and good times, Eccl. 10:19, Hosea 2:11

Feathers-symbolic of covering and protection, Ps. 91:4. A person or creature with feathers within a dream may be an evil spirit

Feet-symbolic of a journey or a messenger. Not having any feet is symbolic of trusting in a fool, Prov. 26:6. Dirty feet are symbolic of sin, Song. 5:3

Fence-to dream of a fence may symbolize a crossable barrier in life. A leaning fence can symbolize a person under pressure, Ps. 62:3. A barbwire fence can symbolize a dangerous obstacle in life

Ferris wheel-symbolic of doing the same things over and over

Ferry-symbolic of something in life that will pass you to your next destination

Festering wound-a symbol of unconfessed sin in a person's life, Ps. 38:5. Festering sores can also be injuries or pain caused by another person

Festival-this is symbolic of joy, thanksgiving and fellowship with other Christians, Ps. 42:4

Fever-a person sick with a fever can be symbolic of a sinful lifestyle, Lev. 26:16

Field-a plowed field is symbolic of a life ready for new things. An empty field is symbolic of an unused portion of your life. A field ready for harvest is symbolic of an upcoming harvest in your life, maturity or evangelism, Matt. 9:37

Field goal kicker-symbolic of a high pressure situation in life in which you play a critical role in determining the outcome

Fig cake-symbolic of intercession and revival, 1 Sam. 25:18, 30:12

Fig tree-to dream of tending a fig tree is symbolic of up-coming honor if the tree is healthy, Prov. 27:18

Fighter jet-symbolic of a fast-paced lifestyle or a symbol of war

Fighting-if you are fighting your relatives in a dream it is symbolic of shame and disgrace, Prov. 19:26. If you fight other people it symbolizes bitterness and anger towards them

Figs-love, goodness, Song. 2:13

Filing cabinet-symbolic of storing events, situations or memories

Fire-symbolic of the word of God, Ps. 29:7, Jer. 23:29. Fire can also symbolize a raging problem in someone's life. Fire, brimstone and scorching winds are all judgments against the wicked, Ps. 11:6. A house on fire is symbolic of judgment, Ezek. 16:41

Fire alarm-a warning of impending trouble in life, Hosea 5:8

Fire breathing-a person breathing fire out of their mouth symbolizes a verbal attack, Ps. 57:4

Fire extinguisher-symbolic of the need to put out an argument or disagreement, Prov. 25:8

Fire walking-to dream of walking or passing through fire is symbolic of being tested, refined or matured, Ps. 66:12, 1 Peter 4:12

Firefighter-a person who helps extinguish problems between people or helps out in times of disaster

Fish-symbolic of Christians, proselytes or other people, Eccl. 9:12, Mark. 1:17, Zeph. 1:10. Fish may also be symbolic of the things you catch from an environment

Fishhook-symbolic of being caught, Job 41:1

Fishnet-symbolic of a large catch, Lk.5:6

Fishtail-to dream of a car fishtailing is symbolic of losing control

Fist-to dream of a fist is symbolic of aggression and anger, Ex. 21:18

Flag-a flag is an emblem of a nation and is given to draw attention to that particular country for prayer. A flag can also be a symbol of God's love and protection for an individual, Ps. 60:4

Flamethrower-symbolic of destructive words, Prov. 16:27

Flat tire-symbolic of not being able to move quickly in life or not being able to go where you want

Flea-a nuisance or minor problem, 1 Sam. 24:14

Fleece-symbolic of testing, faith and approval, Judg. 6:36

Fleeing-symbolic of being pursued by an enemy or God chasing His enemies, Ps. 68:1

Flies-a direct reference to Satan and his kingdom, Isa. 7:18. Dead flies are symbolic of ruin and rottenness, Eccl. 10:1

Flight-swiftness or ease of progress in life, Amos 2:14

Flock-a flock of animals may symbolize great property and wealth, Prov. 27:23

Flood-a great flood or raging flood waters are symbolic of troubles in a person's life or pursuit by an enemy, Ps. 32:6, Ps. 69:1-2. A flood is also symbolic of anger, Prov. 27:4

Flowers-love, marriage, Song. 2:12

Flushing-symbolic of discarding something worthless

Flute-joy, celebration, Ps. 87:7. A flute can also symbolize sorrow depending upon the context within the dream, Jer. 48:36

Fly-ruin, rottenness, Eccl. 10:1. A fly is also symbolic of spiritual or physical enemies, Isa. 7:18

Flying-symbolic of swift progress or a feeling of freedom over obstacles, Jer. 48:9

Flying serpent-symbolic of a deadly, hard to kill or persistent enemy, Isa. 14:29

Fog-something that is short in duration, James 4:14 NLT

Folded hands-symbolic of inaction or sluggishness, Prov. 6:10

Fool's gold-false religion, Col. 2:23

Foot-symbolic of taking a journey. A broken foot can symbolize faithlessness, Prov. 25:19. Having a foot cut off is symbolic of trusting in a foolish person, Prov. 26:6

Football-aggressive living, the game of life

Footprint-following foot prints in a dream is symbolic of following in someone else's path in life. If the foot print is bloody it symbolizes the path of wrongdoers, Hosea 6:8

Footstool-worshiping God, Ps. 99:5. A footstool can also symbolize an enemy being subject to you, Ps. 110:1

Foreskin-an uncircumcised heart can be symbolic of unrepentant sin and rebellion, Jer. 4:4. The foreskin may also symbolize practicing legalism, Gal. 5:2-3

Forest-a forest can be symbolic of an isolated or dangerous place in life, Ps. 104:20

Forest fire-disaster, judgment, Ps. 83:14, Jer. 21:14

Forest ranger-symbolic of a helper

Fortress-symbolic of the protection afforded to believers through faith in Christ, Ps. 31:3. A fortress can also symbolize a strong enemy presence in your life

Fortune teller-a symbol of a person with Satanic influence in your life or a demonic entity wanting to plant a false word in your life, Deut. 18:10

Fountain-a symbol of life or a life giving source, Ps. 36:9

Fox-to dream of a fox is symbolic of a crafty and scheming individual, Lk.13:32

Fox cub-symbolic of tiny problems, Song. 2:15

Frame-to see the frame of a house is symbolic of a person's life being built or a ministry being built, Eph. 4:12-16

Friend-symbolic of help and understanding, Prov. 7:4

Frogs-symbolic of demons or unclean spirits, Rev. 16:13-14

Frontline-symbolic of being at the point of attack in spiritual warfare, 2 Sam. 11:15

Frost-destruction, judgment, Ps. 78:47

Fruit-symbolic of God's blessing upon the earth and Christ's love for His bride, Song. 2:3, Gen. 1:11. Fruit in a dream can also mean results. If the fruit is rotten or spoiled in a dream it symbolizes abandonment, curses and people of bad character, Jer. 24:1-10.

Fumble-symbolic of making a critical mistake

Funeral-symbolic of death or the end of something, Job 21:33 NLT

Funeral procession-symbolic of wailing and mourning over the death of something in your life, Jer. 9:17-19

Furnace-this symbolizes God's judgment upon His enemies, Ps. 21:9

G.

Game-to see yourself playing in a game is symbolic of living life, Heb. 12:1

Gangsters-symbolic of a group of demons, Hosea 7:1

Garbage-symbolic of worthless things. Garbage on your face symbolizes rejection, Mal. 2:3

Garbage truck-symbolic of needing to remove worthless things from your life

Garden-symbolic of love and flourishing, Jer. 31:12, Song. 4:12

Garter snake-a spiritual enemy that is harmless or easily resisted

Gas mask-symbolic of a poisonous environment. If you are wearing a gas mask it symbolizes protection from something harmful

Gasoline-symbolic of charging or energizing a situation, Prov. 26:20

Gate-a gate can be an entry point for angels and demons, Isa. 28:6, Gen. 28:17. If you find yourself at a gate in a dream it can also symbolize a position of council, Gen. 19:1. Closing a gate in a dream is symbolic of shutting someone or something out of a person's life, Mal. 1:10

Gathering-prudent, wise, Prov. 10:5

Gazelle-swiftness, Prov. 6:5. A gazelle is also symbolic of a lover or a fiancé, Song. 2:9

Gecko-unnoticed, small stature, Prov. 30:28

Gems-things of high value (may be spiritual or material) 1 Cor. 3:12

General-symbolic of high command, 1 Sam. 8:12 NLT

Generator-symbolic of a supernatural power source

Giant-a giant is a large spiritual enemy that you will need God's power to overcome, 1 Sam. 17:4

Gifts-symbolic of the love of Christ, Eph. 4:8

Girl Scout-a very helpful and courteous person

Glass-symbolic of clarity and transparency, Rev. 21:18-21

Globe-symbolic of the Earth

Glue-symbolic of peace, Eph. 4:3

Glutton-poverty, Prov. 23:20

Goal keeper-symbolic of resistance

Goat-symbolic of those who do not believe in Christ, Matt. 25:33

God-to dream of God can symbolize a need for instruction on living or an earthly commission, Jer. 1:4-10, Gen. 20:3

Gold-symbolic of wisdom and high quality ministerial work, 1Cor. 3:12

Golden bowl-symbolic of the prayers of the saints, Rev. 5:8

Golden Cup-symbolic of being used by God, Jer. 51:7

Golden image-to dream of a golden object may be symbolic of an idol in someone's life, Ps. 106:19

Golf-playing golf in a dream is symbolic of your life. If you make a hole in one you are doing well. If you are playing poorly it symbolizes a period of disorder in your life

Gong-uncaring or without love, 1 Cor. 13:1

Goodness-symbolic of God's character and the fruit of the Spirit, Gal. 5:22

Gorilla-a looming problem

Government-symbolic of God given authority, Rom. 13:1

Governor-symbolic of authority and rule, Mal. 1:8

Grade-symbolic of how well a person is doing in a certain area in life, James 3:1

Grain-symbolic of God's provision and blessing, Jer. 31:12

Grandchildren-a crown, Prov. 17:6

Grapes-a symbol of something valuable or a prized position, Gen. 40:10-11. If the grapes are sour it symbolizes sin in your life, Jer. 31:30. Sour grapes can also symbolize something that is not ready

Grass-symbolic of the green pastures of God, Ps. 23:2. Withered grass is symbolic of those who do wrong, Ps. 37:2

Grass snake-symbolic of harmless enemies

Grasshopper-old age, Eccl. 12:5

Gravel-symbolic of stolen goods, Prov. 20:17. To have gravel in the mouth is symbolic of being conquered, Lam. 3:16

Gray hair-wisdom, a crown of glory, Prov. 16:31

Grenade-an explosive issue

Grim Reaper-symbolic of death. To see the Grim Reaper can be indicative of a demonic stalker in your life or the life of someone else in the dream

Grinding wheel-symbolic of something that wears you down or kills you slowly

Groom-this is symbolic of Christ or the sun, Ps. 19:5

Ground-symbolic of the readiness of a person to receive the gospel. If the ground is dry it symbolizes spiritual bareness, Hosea 10:12

Growling-a symbol of dissatisfied and wicked people, Ps. 59:15

Guards-symbolic of God's servants, Song. 3:3 or angels, Ps. 91:11. If the guards are dressed in black it can symbolize demonic oppression

Guide-symbolic of God, the Holy Spirit and righteousness, Ps. 23:3

Guitar-worship, melody, joyousness, Ps. 45:8

Gum-chewing gum can symbolize a person's immaturity

Guns (rifles, assault weapons, pistols) to dream of having a gun is symbolic of being armed with the word of God. To have a gun pointed at you is symbolic of being under attack by spiritual enemies or people. Guns are also symbolic of the weapons people use against each other (curses, lies, mischief, slander and insults) Ps. 10:7

Gunslinger-symbolic of being in a battle with spiritual enemies

Gutter-to see someone in a gutter is symbolic of having strayed from the path of righteousness

Gym-symbolic of strengthening the spirit through prayer and reading the Bible. A gym may also symbolize bodily exercise, 1 Tim. 4:8

Gypsy-a gypsy can symbolize a person who travels and never settles down

H.

Hail-destruction, judgment, Ps. 78:47

Hail Mary-symbolic of having long odds for a positive outcome in a situation or a last ditch effort

Hair-long hair is symbolic of femininity, 1 Cor. 11:14-15. Grey hair is symbolic of glory and honor, Prov. 20:29

Half-man-half-animal-to see or speak with a half-man-half-animal creature in a dream is symbolic of a demonic entity attempting to influence your life

Hall-a symbol of a path in life or choices. A long hallway can symbolize a long monotonous journey

Hall of Fame-heroes of the faith, Heb. 12:1

Hammer-the word of God is a hammer, Jer. 23:29. A militant nation can also be a hammer, Jer. 50:23

Hand-a right hand symbolizes God's strength or long life, Ps. 20:6, Prov. 3:16. A left hand symbolizes the riches and honor of wisdom, Prov. 3:16. If the person is evil a hand symbolizes wicked scheming and bribery, Ps. 26:10. An open hand is symbolic of grace, Ps. 123:2

Handcuffs-symbolic of the power to bind or stop certain actions or behavior, Matt. 16:19

Happiness-symbolic of possessing wisdom, Prov. 3:18

Harbor-shelter, Acts 27:12

Harlot-rebellion, loudness, death, Prov. 7:11

Harp-a symbol of joy in the Lord, 43:4

Harvest-symbolic of gathering, Prov. 6:8

Hatchet-smashing, destroying, Ps. 74:6

Hawk-this can be symbolic of a demonic influence in someone's life if the bird is black or grey

Hazard sign-a warning

Head-to dream of something being on your head can be symbolic of God's blessing or a curse, Prov. 10:6. The head is also symbolic of a wise and honorable person, Isa. 9:15. A faceless head can symbolize the flesh and humanity

Health-a symbol of the word of God, Prov. 4:22

Hearse-a hearse symbolizes death or the impending death of a relationship

Heart-a darkened heart or a stone heart is symbolic of a wicked or unregenerate person, Ezek. 36:26. An upside down heart is symbolic of distress and anxiety over troubles in life, Lam. 1:20

Heaven-a symbol of God's glory, Ps. 19:1

Heckler-a scoffer, an ungodly person, Ps. 1:1-2

Hedge-symbolic of God's protection. If the hedge is made of thorns it symbolizes a lazy person, Prov. 15:19

Hedgehog-solitude or separation, Isa. 14:23

Helicopter-a helicopter can symbolize someone who lives a fast paced lifestyle, someone who drinks, parties and uses drugs

Hell-eternal punishment, Matt. 10:28

Helmet-a symbol of salvation, Eph. 6:17

Hemorrhage-symbolic of needing to place your faith in Christ, Lk.8:43

Henna-symbolic of protection, Song. 1:14

Herbs-symbolic of love and goodness, Song. 5:13

Herd-a herd of animals may symbolize the condition of your property or wealth, Prov. 27:23

Heroin (see Drugs)

Hiding-symbolic of a prudent person, Prov. 27:12. Hiding can also symbolize a being fearful

Highway-symbolic of the path of an upright person, Prov. 15:19

Hiking-symbolic of life's journey or the path you are currently on in life

Hill-a hill in a dream may indicate an easily overcome obstacle. A brilliantly lit hill is symbolic of God's dwelling place, Ps. 43:3. A hill can also symbolize a place in life where you can build, work and cultivate good things, Isa. 7:25

Hindu gods-to see a Hindu god in your dream is symbolic of someone who is filled with influences from the East, Isa. 2:6

Hitting-to hit another person in a dream is symbolic of anger directed towards others. If you hit yourself in a dream it is symbolic of regret, Jer. 31:19

Hog-symbolic of worldly people or sinful living, Matt 7:6

Holding hands-this is a symbol of God's faithfulness, protection and love, Ps. 37:24. Holding hands with someone in a dream means being in agreement with them

Hole (open pit) symbolic of a trap or a prostitute, Prov. 23:27, Prov. 28:10

Homeless man-a vagrant may be symbolic of a spiritual enemy, a wanderer

Homerun-success in the game of life

Homosexual-a spirit of perversion, Lev. 18:22-23

Honey-symbolic of the law, teachings, testimony and judgments of the Lord, Ps. 19:7-10

Honeycomb-pleasant speech, kind words, healing, Prov. 16:24

Honking-symbolic of impatience

Hooker-an adulterous woman or a curse, Prov. 23:27

Horn-symbolic of power, boasting and pride, Ps. 75:4-5

Hornet-symbolic of a spirit of terror and confusion, Ex. 23:27-28

Horse-work or war, Prov. 21:3. A white horse is symbolic of Christ's return, Rev. 6:2

Hospital-symbolic of a place of healing

Hotel-to dream of being in a hotel is symbolic of a place of temporary living or employment

Hourglass-symbolic of running out of time or needing to manage your time better

House-symbolic of your life or the place where you live or work, Matt.12:43-44. A person tearing down their own house is symbolic of a fool, Prov.14:1. A crumbling house is symbolic of a wicked person, Prov.14:11. A house filled with good things is symbolic of a wise person, Prov. 21:20. A house made of cards or flimsy material is symbolic of folly. A house on top of sand is symbolic of disaster, Matt. 7:26. A house on fire is symbolic of judgment, Ezek. 16:41

Howling-a symbol of the voice of a wicked person, Ps. 59:6

Hulk-to see the Incredible Hulk in a dream is symbolic of a demonic strongman, Matt. 12:29

Hummingbird-busy, industrious

Hunter-to have the upper hand in a situation, Jer. 16:16

Hurricane-storms symbolize distress and trouble in a person's life, Ps. 107:28-29

Hut-symbolic of placing your trust in something flimsy or unsafe, Lk.6:49

Hyena-symbolic of a person or demon that pursues and harasses people

Hyssop-symbolic of faith in the blood of Christ,
Ex. 12:22

I.

Ice-symbolic of spiritual apathy, Rev. 3:15. Ice under your feet is symbolic of the path of wickedness, Ps. 73:18

Ice cream-joy, happiness, fun

Ice water-refreshing, good news, Prov. 25:25

Iceberg-hidden disaster

ICU (intensive care unit) symbolic of needing major help

Icy path-if you find yourself slipping on an icy path it symbolizes the path of the arrogant and wicked, Ps. 73:18, Jer. 23:12

Idol-to see an idol in a dream is symbolic of stupidity and delusion, Jer. 10:8

Immunization-symbolic of building character and strength to resist temptation

Implant-symbolic of something in your life that did not originate with you

Impound-symbolic of stopping someone's progress in life

Incense-symbolic of prayer, Ps. 141:2

Incest-to dream of an incestuous relationship is indicative of an influence from a spirit of perversion or being around a person who is perverse

Indian (Native American) symbolic of animism and the worship of nature

Infant-symbolic of an early stage of an idea or new thing

Inheritance-symbolic of a good person, Prov. 13:22

Injury (incurable) a symbol of deep-rooted sin in someone's life, Jer. 30:15

Insurance-symbolic of the need to insulate oneself against potential loss

Interior designer-symbolic of someone who has an eye for beauty, art and tasteful things

Investigator-to dream of being a private investigator is symbolic of being noble minded and astute, Acts 17:10-11

Iron-strength or men, Prov. 27:17

Iron bars-symbolic of arguments, Prov. 18:19

Iron rod-symbolic of judgment, Rev. 19:15

Island-a place of temporary, seasonal growth or a symbol of isolation

Israel-to dream of the nation Israel may symbolize a call for prayer over the Middle East

Ivory-symbolic of luxury, Amos 3:15

J.

Jackal-a symbol of an evil scoffer, Ps. 44:19

Jacket-protection or covering

Jail-symbolic of a loss of freedom or being bound and imprisoned mentally or spiritually, Ps. 137:3

Jailer-symbolic of a spiritual oppressor, Matt. 18:34

Janitor-humble circumstances, servitude, an official position of trust, 1 Chron. 9:17-26

Javalina-a devourer, a symbol of a curse upon your valuables or property, Ps. 80:13

Javelin-war, Joshua 8:18

Jawbone-symbolic of supernatural strength, Judg. 15:15

Jaws-large, powerful jaws of an animal or a crushing machine symbolize a trap, Ps. 141:9

Jellybeans-a tempting treat or colorful candy can manifest itself in a dream out of a desire for candies, Isa. 29:8. Jellybeans may also symbolize immaturity in a person

Jester-this can symbolize a slanderer, Ps. 35:15-16

Jesus-to dream of Jesus is symbolic of an invitation to salvation through the blood of Christ, Rom. 10:9-10

Jet-to dream of being in a fighter jet can symbolize a fast, raucous lifestyle, one filled with parties and drug use. To dream of flying on a commercial jet liner can symbolize employment with a large international ministry or company

Jewels-symbolic of the true riches of heaven, 1 Cor. 3:12. Jewels can also symbolize things of earthly value, Prov. 8:10-11

Jogging-symbolic of a relaxing pace in life

Joy-symbolic of God's favor and the fruit of the Spirit, Gal. 5:22

Judge-this is a reference to God or Christ, Ps. 51:4. A judge can also symbolize trouble with earthly authorities

Judges bench-symbolic of the judgment seat of Christ where individuals are accountable for their lives, Rom. 14:10

Juggling-symbolic of being busy or overwhelmed

Jumper cables-symbolic of a connection to a supernatural source of power

Jungle gym-playing around

Junk-symbolic of reading or watching worthless material, Prov. 15:14

Junk food-listening to advice that has little value, Jer. 23:32

Jury-weighing evidence or passing judgment, James 5:9

JV (junior varsity) symbolic of not yet being at the highest level of competition in a particular field of interest

K.

Kamikaze-symbolic of recklessness or something doomed for failure, Deut. 1:43

Kangaroo-symbolic of a relationship or situation that will jump to life if you speak God's word over it

Karate-symbolic of being skilled in spiritual warfare, 2 Cor. 10:4

Keg-symbolic of licentiousness and excess, 1 Pet. 4:3

Kernel-symbolic of small beginnings, Amos 9:9

Keys-symbolic of spiritual authority over the realm of Satan, Matt. 16:19. A key can also be a critical or crucial element to something in life

Kicking-to kick an object in a dream is a symbol of self-regret, Jer. 31:19. To kick at a person in a dream is a symbol of anger directed towards others

Kidnaper-a symbol of being taken somewhere in life against your will. Being kidnapped can also symbolize a demonic presence attempting to steal from you, Jn. 10:10

Killer-to dream of being chased by a killer is symbolic of demonic activity and spiritual enemies, Jn. 10:10

Killing-to see yourself killing someone in a dream may be a result of suppressed anger, fear or jealousy towards that person, Gen. 4:8

Kiln-doing hard, dirty work as a result of sin, 2 Sam. 12:31 NLT

Kindness-symbolic of God's favor and the fruit of the Spirit, Gal. 5:22

King-to dream of being a king can symbolize a position of high status in life. A king is also symbolic of God and Christ, 1 Tim. 6:15, Isa. 43:15

King cobra-symbolic of a demon, Deut. 32:33

Kissing-symbolic of love, affection and intimacy, Song. 1:1-2

Kitchen-home life, serving others or worrying too much, Lk.10:40

KKK (Ku Klux Klan) symbolic of racism and bigotry

Knife-symbolic of weaponry against a perceived enemy, Prov. 23:2. If the knife is dull it symbolizes the need to use God's wisdom, Eccl. 10:10

Knight-symbolic of a person you think highly of or have a romantic interest in

Knocking-symbolic of an invitation, Song. 5:2, Rev. 3:20

KO (knockout) symbolic of winning a fight, 1 Cor. 9:26

L.

Labor (birth) symbolic of intense pain, Jer. 6:24

Labyrinth-this is symbolic of feeling lost or trapped in life

Ladder-a ladder may symbolize moving to a higher spiritual area in life, Gen. 28:12. A ladder may also symbolize promotion on the job

Lake-symbolic of your environment or surroundings. If the water is clear you are in a good place. If the water is dirty or murky you are in a bad environment

Lamb-symbolic of Christ or people, Ps. 78:71

Lamp-this is a reference to the eye and our Christian walk, the Holy Spirit is the oil, Ps. 18:28, Lk.11:34, Matt. 25:1-10. A lamp is also symbolic of the word of God, Ps. 119:105

Lamps-of-fire-symbolic of the seven-fold flow of the Holy Spirit, Isa. 11:2, Rev. 4:5

Lantern-symbolic of the word of God, Ps. 119:105

Laser-high-tech weaponry or end-times wars

Laughing-symbolic of God's superiority over His enemies, Ps. 37:13. Laughing can also mean that you are filled with the joy of the lord. If others are laughing at you in a dream it symbolizes arrogance

Lava-destruction, judgment, Rev. 8:8

Leaf-change or fragility, Job 13:25

Leak-symbolic of pesky problems in your life. A leaky roof may also symbolize idleness, Eccl. 10:18

Leaven-symbolic of hypocrisy, slander or unrighteousness, Matt. 16:6

Leech-greedy person, Prov. 30:15

Left-turning to the left during a dream can symbolize the path of foolishness, Eccl. 10:2

Lemons-bitterness or a situation that is not to your liking, Heb. 12:15

Lens (eye glasses) symbolic of your perspective or opinion

Leopard-symbolic of solitude and seclusion, Song. 4:8. A leopard can also symbolize an ambush by an enemy, Hosea 13:7, Jer. 5:6

Leprosy-symbolic of being treated as an outcast, Lev. 13:45

Letter-writing a letter in a dream is symbolic of telling someone things you wanted to say but never had the chance to do

Leviathan-symbolic of the devil, pride, rebellion, Job 41:1

Library-symbolic of a search for information and a love of knowledge

Licking dust-to dream of someone licking the dust is symbolic of being any enemy of God, Ps. 72:9

Lie detector-symbolic of needing to be honest, Col. 3:9

Life insurance-symbolic of salvation, Titus 2:13

Lifeguard-symbolic of watching out for and protecting others, Ps. 41:1-2

Lifejacket-to see someone throw you a lifejacket in a dream is symbolic of rescue during desperate times, Ps. 6:4

Light-this is a symbol of God or the word of God, Ps. 27:1, Prov. 6:23

Light bulb-to be in the dark and then have a light bulb turn on is symbolic of God showing you that righteous living will illuminate your situation, Isa. 58:9-10

Lighthouse-symbolic of direction in times of trouble

Lightning-symbolic of supernatural power, Ezek. 1:14

Lightning eyes-symbolic of a supernatural being

Lilies-young girls, Song. 2:2. Lilies are also symbolic of blossoming in life, Hosea 14:5

Limp-walking with a limp is symbolic of having been humbled, Gen. 32:25

Limp hands-powerlessness, Jer. 50:43

Lion-this can be the devil, Ps. 10:9. A lion can also reference Jesus, Ps. 17:12. Watch what the lion does in the dream to determine the meaning. If the lion is intimidating and aggressive it is symbolic of a spiritual enemy in your life, 1 Pet. 5:8

Lips-symbolic of a person's speech, Isa. 6:5. If the lips are diseased it symbolizes slander, cursing and abusive speech. If the lips are dripping with honey it can symbolize seductive words, Prov. 5:3

Lipstick-symbolic of beautifying yourself

Litmus paper-symbolic of establishing true character, Prov. 17:3

Lizard-symbolic of a familiar spirit. A lizard may manifest in a dream as a creature with a human face and a nasty disposition that lives in your home

Load-this can be a symbol for a person's sins or anxieties in life, Ps. 38:4, Matt. 11:30. A heavy load can also symbolize other people's problems, Gal. 6:2

Lock-symbolic of something that is sealed or cannot be opened without God's permission, Song. 4:12

Locker room-symbolic of preparation or the time right before a major event in your life

Locusts-symbolic of many enemies, Jer. 51:14. Also symbolic of a large demon army, Rev. 9:3

Log-symbolic of hypocrisy or having problems that you cannot see, Matt. 7:5

Lone wolf-symbolic of an outsider or a person who wants to do everything alone

Long jump-symbolic of reaching for a far-away goal

Looting-symbolic of being overrun by physical or spiritual enemies, Amos 3:11

Love-symbolic of God's character and the fruit of the Spirit, Gal. 5:22

Luggage-symbolic of travel or carrying around things from your past, Matt. 11:28

Lukewarm water-symbolic of spiritual apathy, Rev. 3:15

Lurking-a person lurking in your dream is symbolic of enemies, Ps. 56:6

Lynch mob-symbolic of a group of people who hate you, Acts 16:22 NLT

M.

Machine gun-symbolic of harmful words or spiritual weaponry

Maggot-symbolic of a wicked person, Job 25:6

Magician-a person involved in witchcraft, divination or sorcery symbolizes a person being used by demonic forces to manipulate a situation. A magician is a symbol of fraud and deception, Acts. 13:10

Magnifying glass-examining something or someone intently, 2 Cor. 13:5

Maid-servant hood, Job 19:16

Mailbox-symbolic of someone or God wanting to send you a message

Makeup-symbolic of making yourself beautiful or self-improvement, 2 Kings 9:30

Mall-symbolic of life's choices

Mamba (snake) symbolic of an evil spirit, Isa. 59:4-5

Mane-symbolic of maturity

Manger-symbolic of humble beginnings and the birth of Christ, Lk.2:12

Mantle-responsibility, authority, office, 1 Kings 19:19. The color of the mantle will give you insight into the meaning of the dream

Manuel labor-symbolic of making money or profit, Prov. 14:23

Manure-hard labor, dirty work or being admonished by God, Ezek. 4:12

Map-symbolic of a person's direction in life. If the roads are crooked it symbolizes a sinful lifestyle, Isa. 59:8 NLT

Marching-symbolic of an army, Joel 2:7

Marijuana (see Drugs)

Marionette-symbolic of a person who is controlled by spirits, 1 Kings 22:22-23

Market-symbolic of the world, business and profit, Amos 8:5, Lk.11:43

Marsh-symbolic of the grave, death and destruction, Isa. 14:23 NLT

Mascara-symbolic of beautifying yourself, Jer. 4:30

Mask-someone who has a mask or disguise on during a dream is symbolic of deception, 2 Cor. 11:14

Matador-symbolic of taking chances with your life

Match-symbolic of starting arguments, Prov. 26:20-21

Maze-this is symbolic of being lost or feeling trapped in life

Measuring stick-symbolic of God examining someone or something, Ezek. 40:5

Meat-symbolic of great spiritual truths, 1 Cor. 3:2

Meat hook-symbolic of being dragged off against your will, Amos 4:2

Mecca-Islam, the Middle East

Medical exam-dreaming of a medical exam can be a prophetic warning from God to show you an injury or illness about yourself or others

Medicine-a joyful heart, Prov. 17:22. Medicine can also symbolize a need for prayer and professional medical help

Melting-symbolic of wavering or losing resolve over a situation, Isa. 13:7

Menorah-symbolic of the nation of Israel, Ex. 25:31-40

Menstruation-to dream of menses may result from stress and anxiety or not feeling presentable, Gen. 31:35

Mental hospital-to dream of a psychiatric ward is symbolic of having issues with depression and fear or feeling overwhelmed in life

Mental patient-to dream of a psychotic person may symbolize an out of control lifestyle or a demonic attack on your life

Menu-symbolic of choices

Mercenary-symbolic of a hired specialist. A mercenary is a spiritual enemy who specializes in attacking Christians, Ezra 4:4-5, Deut. 23:4

Merchant-symbolic of buying, selling and making a profit, Ezek. 27:3

Meteor-symbolic of disaster or end-times events, Rev. 8:10

Meth (see Drugs)

Mice-mice can be symbolic of a curse, 1 Sam. 6:4. Mice can also symbolize things that are detestable, Isa. 66:17

Microscope-symbolic of self-examination, Lam. 3:40

Midnight-a reminder to thank and praise God continually, Ps. 119:62. The middle of the night can also be a call to pray and stand on guard against spiritual enemies

Mildew-a curse, Amos 4:9

Mile stone-symbolic of a significant event in life, Josh. 4:1-9

Military uniform-fatigues are symbolic of the Lord's army, a Christian soldier, 2 Tim. 2:3-4

Milk-symbolic of the word of God, 1 peter 2:2

Millstone-symbolic of being weighed down with sin, Isa. 1:4

Mine field-symbolic of hidden dangers

Mining-symbolic of earthly treasures, Job 28:2 NLT

Mint-symbolic of exact giving, Lk.11:42

Mire-being in deep mire is symbolic of coming under an overwhelming attack by your enemies, Ps. 69:2

Mirror-self-examination, James 1:23 or being overly self-conscious

Miscarriage-to dream of an aborted fetus can symbolize a discarded idea in someone's life or the actual event of having aborted a child

Mischief-dreaming of being involved with mischievous acts is symbolic of foolish behavior, Prov. 10:23

Missiles-symbolic of spiritual warfare or end-times events

Missionary-symbolic of ministerial work, Acts 15:36

Mist-symbolic of something temporal, vanishing or fleeting, Prov. 21:6, Hosea 6:4 NLT

Mobsters-symbolic of a group of demons, Hoses 7:1

Mold-rotten, unsalvageable, Amos 4:9

Mole (animal) a mole is symbolic of hiding from trouble, Isa. 2:20

Mole (blemish) symbolic of being self-conscious. If you dream of seeing other people's moles it can symbolize looking at other people's flaws or being judgmental

Monastery-symbolic of seclusion and trying to hide yourself from the world

Money-finding money in a dream may be symbolic of an upcoming financial blessing. If you have a house made of money (dollar bills or coins) it can symbolize trusting in wealth, Prov. 10:15

Monk-symbolic of chastity

Monkey-playfulness, childlike

Monster-a devouring beast is symbolic of a problem or spiritual enemy capable of swallowing your life, Jer. 51:34

Moon-the moon is an ancient symbol for a pagan deity, Deut. 4:19. A full moon is symbolic of the end of a journey, Prov. 7:20. A full moon can also symbolize a time for feasting, joy and praise, Ps. 81:3. The moon may also symbolize something that is established, Jer. 31:35, Ps. 89:37

Mop-symbolic of the need to clean out an area of your life, Gen. 35:2 NLT

Morning-lovingkindness, Ps. 92:2

Mosque-a symbol of Islam

Motel-a motel is symbolic of a transient stay of employment, school or living

Moth-a symbol of transient wealth or something that is consuming your valuables, Ps. 39:11

Motorcycle-symbolic of a fast-paced or free-living lifestyle or individual

Mountain-a large mountain can symbolize the prosperity and favor of God on your life, Ps. 30:6-7. A treacherous or foreboding mountain can symbolize an obstacle or resistance. Moving a mountain can symbolize faith in God, Ps. 125:1. Mountains can also symbolize nations or life's journey, Isa. 2:2, Jer. 51:25

Mourners-death, funeral, Eccl. 12:5

Mouse-a mouse can symbolize the need to sanctify and purify yourself or your surroundings from detestable things, Isa. 66:17

Mouth-a mouth symbolizes your speech or your words. A crooked mouth is symbolic of perverse speech, Prov. 8:8. A silver mouth symbolizes a righteous person, Prov.10:20

Movie-symbolic of being entertained. Movies can also be used to show you something important

Movie Theater-symbolic of being assembled with people of similar interests or activities

Moving van-symbolic of relocation

Mud-if a person is covered in mud it may symbolize being tainted or spotted by sin, Isa. 57:20

Muddy pit-if a person is in a muddy pit it symbolizes a place of destruction, Ps.40:2

Muddy water-this is symbolic of impure doctrine, stagnant living or a spoiled and foul environment, Prov. 25:26

Mule-this animal is symbolic of stubbornness. A mule may also be symbolic of a person or a situation, Ps. 32:9-10

Murder-symbolic of jealousy, injustice and unrighteousness, Isa. 1:21. Murdering people in a dream may also be the result of a demonically induced nightmare

Murderer-a group of murderers is symbolic of a pack of demons, Jn. 8:44

Muscles-to dream of being muscular in a dream may be symbolic of spiritual strength, Matt. 12:29 NLT

Mushroom cloud-nuclear explosions, end-times warfare

Musical notes-symbolic of the way you live your life. If the notes are in harmony it symbolizes virtuous living. If the notes scream it signifies wickedness in your life

Musicians-symbolic of praising God and prophecy, Ps. 68:25, 1 Chron. 25:1

Muslim-symbolic of Islam

Mustard-a symbol of faith, small beginnings and the church, Matt. 13:31-32

Muzzle-a mouth guard against speaking sinful things, Ps. 39:1

Myrrh-symbolic of the death of Christ, Jn. 19:39

Myrtle-symbolic of God's provision in desperate times, Neh. 8:15

N.

Nagging-torment, Judg. 16:16 NLT

Nail polish-symbolic of beautifying yourself

Naked-symbolic of having aspects of your life exposed to other people, Hab. 2:16. If you feel embarrassment it symbolizes a fear of being exposed

Names-to see someone's name in a dream may indicate God's desire for you to pray for them. To see a name crumbling or rotting is a symbol of wickedness and evil, Prov. 10:7

Native American-symbolic of animism and the worship of nature

Nausea-symbolic of a bad environment, a place that will make you sick or bad activities, Prov. 26:11

Nazi-a Nazi soldier symbolizes a spiritual enemy or an oppressive person in your life. A situation in which you need Christ to free you, Acts 10:38

Neanderthal-symbolic of a brutish person

Neck-symbolic of pride, Job 41:22

Necklace-a symbol of something that is close to your heart, Deut. 33:12. If it has a picture of someone in it the necklace symbolizes your love for that person. A necklace is also a symbol of wise instruction and teaching from your parents, Prov. 1:8

Needle (hypodermic) symbolic of drug use

Neighbor-symbolic of the people who live near you. Cursing your neighbor in a dream is symbolic of not having common sense, Prov. 11:12

Nest-a person's home, Prov. 27:8, Job 29:18

Net-a trap laid out by evil, wicked people or spiritual enemies, Ps. 31:4

Newspaper-symbolic of searching for information or staying knowledgeable

Night-symbolic of danger or an enemy, Job 24:14, Ps. 55:10. Night can also symbolize worldly living, Jn. 8:12

Nightclub-symbolic of foolish behavior, Eccl. 7:4

Ninja-a black clad ninja is symbolic of a special demonic envoy with an assignment to kill, steal and destroy, Jn. 10:10

Noah's ark-symbolic of God's promise of safety and provision, Gen. 7:1

Noon-brightness at noon symbolizes God's blessing, Job 11:17

Noose-symbolic of a trap awaiting the wicked, Job 18:10

North-symbolic of the recesses of heaven, Isa. 14:13

Northern army-symbolic of a heavenly army, Joel 2:20

Nose-to dream of a large or pronounced nose is symbolic of someone who is offensively snoopy or curious. Pressing someone's nose in a dream is symbolic of stirring-up strife, Prov. 30:33

Nosedive-symbolic of an unexpected loss of position, status or money, Prov. 28:14-18

Nostrils-dreaming of large nostrils may indicate a person who is self-conscious about their appearance

Notation-symbolic of your actions in life. If your life is not virtuous the notes will scream or sound out of tune

Nuclear war-to dream of nuclear war is symbolic of end-time events, Rev. 6:8

Nude (see Naked)

Nun-symbolic of piety or dedication to God, 1 Cor. 7:32-34

Nurse-a nurse symbolizes caring and helping, Lk.10:34. If you dream of being a nurse it can symbolize your expert role in being used by God to assist someone

Nursing-symbolic of caring for new Christians or nurturing a new thing in your life, 1 Thess. 2:7

Nuts-symbolic of the blessing of God and the best of the land, Gen. 43:11

O.

Oak-symbolic of strength, Amos 2:9

Oasis-symbolic of the peace of Christ during a time of trouble, Ex. 15:27 NLT

Obese-seeing yourself as fat or overweight in a dream can symbolize low self esteem

Occult-symbolic of demonic influences, 2 Kings 9:22

Ocean-if you are in a boat the ocean may be a symbol of the journey of life. If you are swimming in the ocean it can symbolize exploring deep places in life. A stormy or raging ocean is symbolic of the nations, Ps. 65:7

Odor-a foul odor can symbolize a curse, Amos 4:10. A pleasing scent can symbolize goodness and a pleasing life, Eph. 5:2

Office-symbolic of earthly or spiritual authority, 1 Chron. 9:22

Officer-symbolic of leadership or a commission from God, Prov. 6:7

Ogre-symbolic of a wicked, abusive person or a spiritual oppressor

Oil-the Holy Spirit, Matt. 25:1-10. Oil is also an anointing from God, Ps. 23:5, joy, Ps. 45:7

Oil (black crude), gushing oil is symbolic of someone coming into a significant amount of money

Oil derrick-symbolic of generating wealth

Ointment-a good reputation, Eccl. 7:1

Old age-symbolic of God's blessing, Eph. 6:1

Olive branch-symbolic of adoption into God's family, Rom. 11:17

Olive tree-a symbol of end-times witnesses, power, Israel and believers, Rom. 11:24, Rev. 11:4. A green olive tree is symbolic of a prosperous Christian, Ps. 52:8

Olympics-symbolic of competition at a high level or performing well as a Christian, Heb. 12:1

Omega-symbolic of Christ, Rev. 1:8

Onyx-symbolic of Christ's protection and watching out for His people, Ex.25:7

Orchard-symbolic of romantic love, Song. 4:13

Orgy-to dream of an orgy is indicative of an influence from a demonic spirit of perversion, Rom. 13:13 NLT

Orphan-symbolic of Christian duty, Deuteronomy 10:18

Orphanage-symbolic of a call to minister, pray or support orphans, James 1:27

Ostrich-harmless or lacking good sense, Lam. 4:3

Ouija board-symbolic of demonic influence, Ezek. 21:21

Outer space-vastness, separation, Gen. 1:7, Ps. 19:1-3

Oven-this symbolizes God's judgment upon His enemies, Ps. 21:9. An oven can also symbolize an angry heart, Hosea 7:6

Overtime-symbolic of a high pressure period in life in which you play a critical role

Owl-owls can be an evil spirit disguised as a spirit guide, Lev. 11:13-18

Ox-symbolic of slaughter, Prov. 7:22 or strength, Prov. 14:4

Oyster-love, romance, something of great worth

P.

Paddle-symbolic of discipline, Prov. 13:24

Paint-symbolic of covering something, Matt. 23:27. The color of the paint will tell you more about the meaning of your dream

Painting-a symbol of artistic value. The picture in the painting will give you more insight into its meaning

Pale horse-symbolic of death, Rev. 6:8

Pallbearer-symbolic of death and mortality, Eccl. 12:5 NLT

Palm reading-symbolic of witchcraft, Lev. 20:6

Palm tree-symbolic of peace or a person, Song. 7:8. Palm trees are also symbolic of flourishing, Ps. 92:12

Panther-symbolic of lurking evil

Paparazzi-symbolic of worshiping idols or deifying people

Parachute-symbolic of looking for safety during a crisis. If the parachute does not open correctly or has holes in it this means that what you think will keep you safe during a life crisis is not going to protect you

Parade-symbolic of victory in battle, 1 Cor. 4:9 NLT. A parade can also symbolize needless pomp, Isa. 1:12 NLT

Paramedic-symbolic of help in a time of emergency

Parent-symbolic of authority, Deut. 5:16

Park-symbolic of leisurely ease, the beauty of the earth and the futility of living without Christ, Eccl. 2:1-5 NLT

Parrot-symbolic of a person of colorful character or one who repeats what they hear

Passenger-symbolic of being someone's friend or going along with other people's decisions for your life

Passport-symbolic of international travel

Pastries-symbolic of gossip, Prov. 18:8

Pasture-symbolic of peace in life, Ps. 95:7

Patch-symbolic of the need for a renewing of the Holy Spirit, Matt. 9:15-17

Path-a level path is symbolic of walking in God's truth, Ps. 27:11, Jer. 31:9. A hidden path can symbolize an unseen option in life

Patience-symbolic of God's favor and the fruit of the Spirit, Gal. 5:22

Pawnshop-seeing yourself pawn your property in a dream is symbolic of the path to poverty, Ps. 109:11 NLT

Paycheck-symbolic of financial blessing or the wages of your lifestyle, Rom. 6:23. If the check say's "righteousness" it means you are living life rightly. If the check say's "punishment" it symbolizes wicked living, Prov. 10:16

Peace-the feeling of peace in a dream is a blessing from the Lord, Ps.29:1. Peace is also symbolic of God's favor and the fruit of the Spirit, Gal. 5:22

Peaches-a symbol of romantic aspirations and love

Peacock-symbolic of luxury items or showiness, 1 Kings 10:22

Pearl-the gospel or something valuable, Matt. 7:6, 13:45

Peeing (see Urination)

Pelican-distress, affliction, Ps. 102.6

Pen-a symbol of praise, Ps. 45:1

Penny- symbolic of giving out of poverty, Mk. 12:42

Pentagram- symbolic of Occult influences

Perfume-the smell of perfume in a dream is a symbol of the fragrant presence of Christ, Song. 3:6

Peroxide-symbolic of the healing process

Pesticide-symbolic of saturating a problem with wide-ranging prayers

Pestilence-a symbol of God's judgment on sin, Ps. 38:11, Rev. 2:23

Phantom-a ghostly visitor is a demonic presence. A phantom can also suggest that an old issue is still lingering in your life

Pharaoh-symbolic of a hard heart and pride, Ps. 136:15

Phone-symbolic of receiving a message or needing to talk with someone in life

Photographer-symbolic of making memories for others

Physician-a symbol of Christ or a pastor. If you are the physician in a dream it can symbolize a role you fill in the lives of others as healer, comforter and counselor, Jer. 8:22

Picture-to see a picture of someone in a dream is a way to subconsciously bring attention to the person or image within that picture

Pig-symbolic of ungrateful people, mockers and scoffers, Matt 7:6

Pig's snout-if the snout has a gold ring in it this symbolizes a woman without discretion, Prov.11:22

Piggybank-symbolic of saving money or using what you have saved to help others, 1 Cor. 16:2

Pillar-a symbol of responsibility, support and strength, Jer. 1:18. Pillars are also elders or mature Christians, Gal. 2:9

Pilot-dreaming of piloting an aircraft is symbolic of a fast-paced lifestyle. Piloting a commercial jet liner is symbolic of leadership in an international ministry or company

Pinion-symbolic of God's faithfulness and protection, Ps. 91:4

Piranha-symbolic of a large group of spiritual enemies

Pirate-symbolic of a thief or bandit, an outcast from society, Judg. 11:3

Pirate flag-symbolic of an impending attack upon your life or another person's life

Pistol-symbolic of being armed for a fight. The bullets are symbolic of your words, Ps. 10:7. A blank or empty cartridge is symbolic of ineffective prayer

Pit-a hole in the ground is symbolic of a trap or a prostitute, Prov. 23:27, Prov.28:10

Pit-bull-symbolic of tenacity and ferocity

Pitcher (container) symbolic of a person's lungs, Eccl. 12:6

Pizza-a frozen pizza symbolizes unpreparedness

Plague-a symbol of God's judgment on sin, Ps. 38:11, Rev. 2:23

Plane-this can symbolize a world-wide ministry for a Christian or a fast-paced lifestyle for a non-believer

Planting-symbolic of instigating something good or bad depending upon what is being planted. If you dream of planting and sowing fruit or vegetable seeds it symbolizes God's blessing, Ps. 107:37-38

Plants-symbolic of sons, people or the repercussions of your actions, Ps. 144:12. If the plants are withered it symbolizes a lack of vibrancy

Plastic-a symbol of something flexible or pliable

Platoon-symbolic of a group of Christians with the same tactical purpose in spiritual warfare

Playground-symbolic of having fun

Playing field-symbolic of contested territory

Plaza-symbolic of crying out or speaking to people, Amos 5:16

Plow-symbolic of hard, Christian work, 1 Cor. 9:10

Plumbing-symbolic of hard and dirty work

Poison-symbolic of bad activities, negative beliefs and evil things in your life, Jer. 8:14. Poison can also be symbolic of grief, Job 6:4. Wicked words are also symbolic of poison, Ps. 140:3

Poker (card game) symbolic of taking a risk. If you have a good hand it symbolizes having an advantage in a situation. If you have low value cards it symbolizes a need to make peace with your opponent

Polar bear-symbolic of a large problem

Police-symbolic of authority, 1 Pet. 2:13 NLT. Running from the police can be symbolic of having trouble with authority figures in life

Polishing-symbolic of preparation and refinement, Ezek. 21:11 NLT

Pollution-symbolic of grievous sins within a nation or a person's life, Ps. 106:38

Polygraph machine-symbolic of needing to be truthful, Col. 3:9 NLT

Pomegranates-beauty and ministry, Song. 4:3, Ex. 28:34

Pompousness-symbolic of a person without any understanding of God, Ps. 49:20

Pond-a small area or place in life where people come together (church, work or social club)

Pool-symbolic of a place where people gather in life. If the water is dirty it symbolizes wickedness

Pool-hall-symbolic of people trying to scam or deceive you

Pornography-dreaming of pornographic material can symbolize being influenced by a spirit of perversion or coming into contact with someone who is sexually perverse. Pornographic dreams are also caused by looking at sexually explicit films

Port-to see yourself at a port in a dream can be symbolic of running away from God's call on your life, Jn. 1:3 NLT

Port-o-potty-symbolic of bad jokes and bathroom humor

Possession-the sensation of spiritual possession in a dream is symbolic of demonic influences in your life, Mk. 3:11

Postman-symbolic of a messenger. The contents of the letter may be a reminder to pray over the good and bad news you receive in life, 2 Kings 19:14

Pot (Marijuana) dreaming about smoking pot can be an effect of having a current or former drug addiction. Being around people who smoke pot even if you do not can also stir your subconscious to dream about the event

Pothole-symbolic of a rough path or trouble in life, Prov. 10:9 NLT

Potsherd-symbolic of total destruction, Jer. 19:11

Potter's wheel-symbolic of being molded or shaped, Jer. 18:6 NLT

Pottery-symbolic of a godly vessel, Isa. 64:8. If you see broken pottery it means you have lost your strength, Ps. 22:15

Praise-singing to the Lord in a dream symbolizes a godly person, Ps. 30:4

Prayer-praying in a dream is symbolic of the need to pray to Christ, Rom. 10:11

Preacher-a preacher is symbolic of religion. The character of the preacher can be either good or bad depending on the context of the dream, Jude 1:12 NLT

Pregnancy-pregnancy can be literal or figurative. Pregnancy is many times symbolic of conceiving an idea, travailing in its inception and giving birth to a new thing, Isa. 66:9

Prescription-symbolic of instructions for healing or getting better in an area of your life, Isa. 38:21 NLT

Preservatives-jars filled with jams and jellies can be used to imply the preservation of people through God's love, kindness and truth, Ps.40:11

Pressure-a symbol of God's correction and discipline, Ps. 38:2. Pressure can also be a demonic hindrance in your life if the dream is a nightmare

Prince-a prince is symbolic of Christ, Acts 3:15. A dark prince is a symbol of Satan, Eph. 2:2

Princess-to dream of being a princess is symbolic of the royal position of a Christian woman, Ps. 45:9. A princess can also symbolize a difficult woman

Principal-symbolic of authority, 1 Pet. 2:13 NLT

Prison-to dream of being in prison may symbolize not having any hope or joy in life, Ps. 107:10

Prisoner-symbolic of being bound by depression, anxiety or sinful habits, Ps. 146:7

Prostitute-symbolic of the path of death, Prov. 2:16-18

Psychic-dreaming of a psychic giving you information is symbolic of demonic influences trying to direct your life, Lev. 20:6

Puppet-symbolic of someone who is controlled by other people or by demonic influences, Jer. 2:8

Pyramid-a pyramid is symbolic of climbing or reaching for worldly goals rather than having godly aspirations, Heb. 11:26, Jude 1:5

Python-a spirit of divination, related to drug use, murder, theft and mockery. The python is symbolic of a very large demonic entity capable of killing a person, Acts 16:16.

Q.

Q-tip-a metaphorical symbol of a person's need to clean out their ears and listen to good advice, Isa. 6:10

Quacking-symbolic of complaining, harsh or annoying speech

Quarterback-symbolic of leadership

Queen-a symbol of high status in a social group, Ps. 45:9

Queen bee-symbolic of an aggressive or domineering woman, a Jezebel spirit, Rev. 2:20

Quicksand-symbolic of a trap that can kill you, Ps. 69:2

Quiz-symbolic of a short season or period of time in which you are tested, 2 Cor. 8:22

R.

Rabbit-a pagan symbol of fertility. A demon can manifest itself in dreams as a spirit guide with a human body and rabbit head. The rabbit was an unclean animal under the Law, Lev. 11:6

Rabbit's foot-symbolic of false hope

Raccoon-a rascally individual, one prone to foolish behavior

Race-symbolic of the journey of life, Eccl. 9:11

Raft-symbolic of safety in times of trouble

Rags-symbolic of dead works, Isa. 64:6

Rain-a peaceful shower is symbolic of the presence of the Holy Spirit, Ps. 72:6. A driving rain is symbolic of a storm in your life. Raining fire is symbolic of judgment, Ps. 11:6

Rainbow-this is a sign of God's covenant with all life. Rainbows also stand for faithfulness and love, Gen. 9:13

Raisin-symbolic of intercession and revival, 1 Sam. 25:18, 30:12

Raisin cake-love, refreshing, Song. 2:5, 1 Sam. 30:12

Rambo-to dream of being Rambo is symbolic of attacking spiritual enemies by yourself, Deut. 1:44, Ps. 118:12

Rape-to dream of being sexually assaulted is indicative of a demonically induced nightmare

Rapids-this is a symbol of a fast paced or out of control situation

Rapist-symbolic of the devil's desire to take things from people without their consent

Rat-symbolic of a person with low character, morals and ethics

Rattle snake-symbolic of strife, Isa. 59:5

Raven-symbolic of a messenger, Gen. 8:7. A raven can also be a demonic spirit depending on the context of the dream

Raw meat-symbolic of the need for diligence and preparation. Someone eating raw meat is symbolic of laziness, Prov. 12:27

Razor-a symbol of lies, deceit and destruction, Ps. 52:2

Recliner-symbolic of relaxing

Red Cross-symbolic of Christian service or belonging to Christ

Red eyes-symbolic of fatigue from drinking alcohol, Prov. 23:29. Red-eyed creatures in a dream are also symbolic of demonic entities

Red horse-symbolic of war, Rev. 6:4

Red tape-symbolic of a long process in getting something accomplished

Reed-symbolic of the fear of people's perceptions and opinions, Matt. 11:7

Referee-symbolic of Christ, a person of authority or a mediator

Reflection-symbolic of looking into your heart, Prov. 27:19

Refuge-a symbol of God's promises, Ps. 46:1

Relatives-living relatives are symbolic of your current living situation. Dead relatives can be showing you the root of generational blessings or curses in your life, Ex. 34:7

Relay race-symbolic of working as a team

Remote control-control over an aspect of your life or other people's lives

Reporter-symbolic of disseminating information for other people

Reptile-symbolic of an evil spirit, Lev. 11:29-30

Reservoir-a waterless reservoir is symbolic of putting your trust in something other than God, Jer. 2:13

Resistance-a person who resists you in a dream symbolizes a spiritual or physical impediment

Resurrection-symbolic of spiritual awakenings, Jn. 11:25

Revolver-symbolic of being armed with the word of God

Rib-a reminder of a man's relationship to his wife, Gen. 2:22

Ribbons-symbolic of celebration

Riddle-to dream of someone telling you riddles is symbolic of mysteries, Ps. 49:4

Rifle-a symbol of attacking someone with words or being armed with the word of God against an enemy

Right turn-to see a right-turn sign is symbolic of turning towards wisdom, Eccl. 10:2

Ring-to see a ring in a dream can symbolize God's approval and authority, Jer. 22:24, Hag. 2:23

Riot-symbolic of rebellion or a spirit of lawlessness, Acts 19:40

River-symbolic of life's journey. If the river is raging it symbolizes turmoil and distress. If the river is peaceful it symbolizes God's blessing, Deut. 8:7. A dry river can symbolize disappointment, Job 6:15-20. A river can also symbolize the Holy Spirit, Jn. 7:38-39

Road-symbolic of a person's journey in life or a choice. If the road is bumpy and hard it can symbolize a rough period in life. If the road is smooth it symbolizes God's intervention on your behalf, Lk.3:5

Roadblock-symbolic of not being able to move towards a goal, Lam. 3:9

Road sign-a marker for direction in life, Jer. 31:21

Roadrunner-speed, swiftness

Roaring-to hear the roar of an animal in a dream may symbolize a warning of impending danger or being a defenseless victim, Amos 1:2, Jer. 2:14-15

Robbed-to have your property stolen during a dream may indicate a spiritual thief, Jn. 10:10

Robber-symbolic of an evil person, demonic activity in someone's life or an adulterer, Prov. 23:28

Robes-to wear a gold, blue, purple or scarlet robe in a dream is symbolic of holiness, glory and beauty, Ex. 28:2. If the robe is white it means righteousness. If the robe is spotted it means sin is in your life, Zech. 3:1-4

Robin-being obedient to God's commands, Jer. 8:7

Robots-symbolic of future technologies

Rock-this is symbolic of Christ, refuge, a stronghold and strength, Ps. 31:1-3, Ps. 28:1

Rocket-a rocket can be a symbol for a quick and sudden departure from one area of life to a new one

Rod-symbolic of the words of Christ, Isa. 11:4

Roll bar-symbolic of safety from disaster

Roller coaster-symbolic of the ups and downs of life

Roof-a leaking roof is symbolic of idleness. A damaged roof is symbolic of laziness, Eccl. 10:18

Room-to dream of rooms filled with good things symbolizes a person with knowledge, Prov. 24:4. A dirty room symbolizes a person's lifestyle, Matt. 12:44

Rooster-pride, confidence, Prov. 30:31 Matt. 26:34

Root-a symbol of a righteous person, Prov. 12:3. A root can also be the cause of something. If the root has fruit it symbolizes a good person. If the root is dry it symbolizes evil, Hosea 9:16, A root is also symbolic of being firmly planted, Jer. 12:2

Rope-to be tied up in a dream may symbolize sin, Prov. 5:22. A three cord rope symbolizes strength, Eccl. 4:12

Rosary-symbolic of piety and prayers

Rose-a symbol of great beauty and value. A rose can also symbolize our relationship with Christ, Song. 2:1-2

Rotting fruit-symbolic of decay, Job 13:28

Roulette-symbolic of hoping for an unlikely outcome in a situation

Rowing-symbolic of doing hard work in the face of opposition, Mk. 6:48

Rubbing-to dream of someone rubbing you can symbolize sensuousness or an unwanted advance from another person

Rubble-symbolic of calamity, Job 30:24

Rubies-symbolic of something of great worth in life, something set on display, Isa. 54:12

Rugby-symbolic of playing in the game of life

Ruins-judgment, desolation, destruction, Mal. 1:4

Running-if you are running a race it symbolizes doing well in life, Phil. 2:16

Rust-symbolic of earthly riches, Matt. 6:19. Rust is a symbol of all things temporal

S.

Sackcloth-a symbol of mourning, fasting and prayer, Ps. 35:13

Safe (lock box) symbolic of having something secured or out of danger

Sails-symbolic of the empowering of the Holy Spirit or prophecy, 2 Peter 1:21

Salesman-symbolic of persuasion

Salt-a symbol of Christian character, a person who applies the word of God to their life, Matt. 5:13

Salt-flats-symbolic of desolation and abandonment, Ps. 107:34

Salt-pit-symbolic of desolation and destruction, Zeph. 2:9

Sand-immeasurability, Ps. 139:18. Sand is also symbolic of long life, Job 29:18. Sand can also symbolize God's loving thoughts about his children, Ps. 139:17-19

Sandals-symbolic of the gospel, Eph. 6:11. Sandals are also symbolic of God's love for his wayward children, Lk. 15:21-24

Sandstorm-symbolic of troubles or trials in life, Ps. 83:13-15

Sap-emblematic of being full of life, Ps. 92:14

Sapphire-symbolic of something of high value, Job 28:16

Sasquatch-symbolic of a large problem in your life like depression or anger

Satan-to dream of Satan is symbolic of demonic activity over an area of your life or someone else's life, Acts 26:18, 1 Cor. 5:5

Saw-symbolic of cutting or tearing down by the power of God, Isa. 10:34

Scabs-symbolic of affliction, Isa. 3:17

Scaffolding-symbolic of a work in progress

Scale (reptilian) symbolic of great pride, Job 41:15

Scales (measuring) to dream of a measuring scale or the scales of justice is symbolic of weighing or inspecting the worth and value of a person or object, Ps. 62:9

Scar-symbolic of past hurts, emotional wounds or the need for faith in Christ, Jn. 20:27

Scarecrow-symbolic of putting your trust in something that cannot help you, Jer. 10:5

Scepter-a symbol of authority, sovereignty and rule, Ps. 45:6

School-symbolic of a time of learning in life, Acts 19:9. A school is a common dream setting for past or present important events in a person's life

Scientist-symbolic of analyzing, testing and examining

Scissors-symbolic of the need to cut things out of your life

Scorpion-a scorpion is the equivalent of a snake or a spider. In a dream scorpions represent demons, Lk. 10:19

Screws-symbolic of the need to get something in order or tighten up an area of your life

Scroll-this is symbolic of a specific word from God that carries with it instructions for an earthly commission, Ezek. 3:1

Sea-the sea can be symbolic of many nations and people groups, Ps. 65:5-7. The sea can also symbolize a person's current situation in life

Sea monster-symbolic of a demonic entity or Satanic attack on your life, Ps. 74:13

Séance-if you are participating in a séance during a dream it is a warning that you have become involved with the Occult. If you see other people conducting a séance during a dream it symbolizes people with ties to the Occult attempting to influence your life

Seat-symbolic of a person's social rank or a person's right to occupy a place within a group, 1 Sam. 2:8

Secretary-symbolic of assisting in God's work, Rom. 16:22. Secretaries can symbolize a position as gatekeeper to information and people of authority

Security guard-symbolic of authority, 1 Chron. 9:27

Sediment-the liquid remnants considered worthless. Symbolic of being undisturbed, Jer. 48:11

Seeds-children, the word of God or an investment, Ps. 89:4

Seizure-an epileptic seizure may symbolize demonic oppression in someone's life, Matt. 17:15-18

Self-portrait-to dream of your own picture is symbolic of self-examination

Selling-if a person is selling grain it symbolizes a blessing from God. A person refusing to sell you something you need is symbolic of a hated person, Prov. 11:26

Sepulcher-symbolic of death and resurrection, Matt. 27:52

Serial Killer-symbolic of a demon tasked with trying to take your life, Jn. 10:10

Serpent-to see a serpent in a dream is symbolic of Satan or demons, Rev 12:9. Serpents are lying spirits and spirits of confusion, Isa. 59:4-5

Sewer-symbolic of a bad environment

Sex-to dream of sexual intercourse may be the result of having contact with a person influenced by a spirit of perversion. Sexual content in a dream may also result from being in a relationship with someone past or present. Even if a person is not sexually active it is possible that having a conversation about sex can trigger a sexually explicit dream

Shack-a flimsy life, not trusting in God, Job 27:18

Shackles-affliction, bondage, oppression, Nah. 1:13

Shade-symbolic of protection, Ps. 121:5

Shadow-symbolic of being in the presence of God, Ps. 36:7. A shadow can symbolize a demonic presence or death depending on the emotion associated with the dream, Ps. 44:19, Ps. 23:4

Shaking-symbolic of fear, Isa. 7:2

Shaking hands-symbolic of agreement

Shark-a shark is a symbol of a demonic force or a person with the ability to cause you tremendous harm. Sharks are symbols of a devouring entity

Shattered cups (jars and dishware) these can symbolize ruin and destruction, Jer. 48:12

Shaving-to dream of shaving your legs or face may symbolize a desire to keep your appearance neat and clean at all times. Cutting yourself while shaving may symbolize anxiety associated with trying to groom yourself

Shawl-symbolic of being covered by God or someone in authority, Song. 5:7

Sheep-symbolic of people who belong to Christ, Jn. 10:15

Sheets-clean, fragrant bed sheets are symbolic of virtuous living, Prov. 7:17. Dirty bed linens are symbolic of sinful activities, Ezek. 23:17

Shelter-a place of refuge provided by God from spiritual enemies and people who spread strife, Ps. 31:20

Shelves-symbolic of things you need to put away for a season

Shepherd-this is a reference to Christ or a pastor, Ps. 23:1

Shield-symbolizes faith in Christ and God's faithfulness to His servants, Eph. 6:16, Ps. 28:7. A small shield is symbolic of God's arsenal of weapons against His enemies, Ps. 35:2

Shining face-a symbol of God's blessing, Ps. 67:1

Ship-symbolic of a person's life, James 3:4

Shipwreck-symbolic of a disaster in life, 1 Tim. 1:19

Shoes-symbolic of a servant, Ps. 108:9. Shoes can also symbolize a journey or a person prepared to witness the gospel of Christ, Eph. 6:15

Shopping-symbolic of choices

Short-to be small in stature in a dream is symbolic of feeling unimportant, 1Sam. 15:17. To see others as short is symbolic of feeling superior to other people

Shot-being shot or shooting someone is symbolic of hurtful words (curses, lies, mischief, slander and insults) Ps. 10:7

Shoulders-strength, Eccl. 12:3, or government, Isa. 9:6. A dislocated shoulder is symbolic of calamity, Job 31:22-23

Shove-to push someone in a dream is symbolic of aggression and anger, Ps. 118:13

Shovel-symbolic of doing hard work

Shower-being in the shower or seeing someone shower in a dream is a symbol of exposure or intimacy

Shrine-symbolic of idol worship, Ezek. 16:24

Sick-to dream of being sick may symbolize a sinful lifestyle or an environment that is bad for you, Rev. 2:22

Sickle-harvesting, Joel 3:13

Siege works-weapons used to besiege a wall or city are symbolic of being involved in a long, drawn-out spiritual battle, Deut. 20:20

Signaling-winking, pointing and signaling others with your feet can symbolize an underhanded person, Prov. 6:13

Signet ring-symbolic of God's approval and authority, Jer. 22:24

Signs-symbolic of looking for directions or needing direction in life, Jer. 31:21

Silence-symbolic of a wise person, Prov. 10:19

Silver-symbolic of pure words and the truth of God, Ps. 12:6. Silver can also mean a high quality ministry, 1Cor. 3:12

Silver cord-symbolic of a person's spinal column, Eccl. 12:6

Simulator-a flight simulator is symbolic of being trained to do a highly skilled activity

Singing-this symbolizes thankfulness to God, Ps. 28:7

Sinking-the sensation of sinking is symbolic of dying, disaster or trouble in life, Jer. 51:64

Sinking ship-to dream of being on a sinking ship symbolizes trouble, failing or impending disaster in your life, 1 Tim. 1:19

Sirens-symbolic of a warning, Num. 10:9

Sister-symbolic of wisdom, Prov. 7:4

Skating-symbolic of enjoying life

Skeleton-symbolic of death. If you are kissing a skeleton in a dream it means you hate wisdom and love death, Prov. 8:36

Skipping-symbolic of childlike behavior, Job 21:11

Skirt-to see someone's skirt lifted up in a dream is symbolic of public humiliation and having weaknesses exposed, Nah. 3:5

Skull-symbolic of death, Prov. 8:36

Sky-symbolic of separation, Gen 1:6. A dark sky means trouble. A clear sky means peace. A red sky means judgment or war. A purple sky can symbolize the second coming of Christ. The sky can also symbolize witness and faithfulness, Ps. 89:37

Skydiving-symbolic of free-fall in life. If you have a parachute it symbolizes a safe landing. If your chute will not open it symbolizes putting your hopes in something that will not help you

Slam dunk-symbolic of performing well in life

Slap-contempt, Job 16:10

Slaughter house-symbolic of being butchered mentally or physically by someone

Slavery-a symbol of oppression, bondage and sin, Deut. 6:12

Sleeping-sleeping during a dream may be symbolic of peace or rest from troubles in your life, Prov.19:23. Sleeping while others are working is symbolic of shame, poverty and unwise behavior, Prov. 10:5

Sleeping bag-symbolic of travel or not having a permanent home, Jer. 10:17

Slingshot-symbolic of fighting spiritual enemies, 1 Sam. 17:50

Slippery path-symbolic of judgment upon the wicked, Ps. 73:18or the way of the wicked, Ps.35:6, Ps. 73:18. Also symbolic of calamity and punishment for wicked behavior, Jer. 23:12

Slipping-symbolic of being envious of arrogant and wicked people, Ps. 73:2-3

Slithering-to dream of someone slithering is symbolic of demonic influences in that person's life

Smelter-symbolic of being tested, Prov. 17:3

Smiling-symbolic of a joyous heart, Prov. 15:13

Smoke-symbolic of an irritating, lazy servant, Prov. 10:26. Smoke is also symbolic of how quickly the wicked vanish from their prosperous position, Ps. 37. 16-20

Smooth tongue-adultery, Prov. 6:24

Snail-a symbol of a wicked person, Ps. 58:8. Snails can also symbolize slowness

Snake charmer-to dream of a snake charmer is indicative of needing to be skillful, cautious and wise, Eccl. 10:11

Snakes-symbolic of lying spirits and spirits of confusion, Isa. 59:4-5. Adders are symbolic of spiritual or physical enemies, Jer. 8:17. In Ps. 140:1-3 it says viper poison comes from a person's mouth. A flying snake is a false religious spirit, a deadly, difficult to kill problem, Isa. 14:29

Snow-a symbol of peace, calm, serenity, purity and cleanness, Ps. 51:7. A blizzard is symbolic of blindness in a situation or resistance in life

Soap-cleansing, Mal. 3:2

Soccer-the game of life or a contest of wills against another group of people

Soft drink-symbolic of refreshing or craving sweets

Soil-symbolic of the condition of a person's heart, Matt. 13:23. Stones in the soil are symbolic of things that need to be removed from a person's life

Soldiers-symbolic of being in Christian service, 2 Tim. 2:3. Soldiers may also symbolize spiritual enemies, Eph. 6:12

Soot-desolation, curse, depravation, Lam. 4:8

Sorcerer-symbolic of demonic influences, Ex. 7:11

Sore-a symbol of unconfessed sin in a person's life, Ps. 38:5, Jer. 30:13. Sores can be emotional injuries or pain caused by another person that hasn't healed

Sour-a sour fruit or taste is symbolic of sin or doing wrong things, Jer. 31:30

South-symbolic of approaching storms, Job 37:9

Sowing clothes-symbolic of a good wife or an industrious person, Prov. 31:22

Sowing machine-symbolic of good deeds towards others, Acts 9:39

Sowing seeds-to dream of sowing fruit and vegetable seeds can symbolize God's blessing, Ps. 107:37-38

Space-symbolic of separation, Gen. 1:6 NLT

Spaceship-a metaphor for a speedy departure, leaving a job or living situation for another very quickly

Spanking-symbolic of discipline, Prov.13:24

Sparkplug-symbolic of igniting spiritual desires

Sparrow-symbolic of God's provision, Matt. 10:29

Spear-a symbol of God's weaponry against His enemies, Ps. 35:3. A spear tip can also be symbolic of the point of attack

Sphere-symbolic of a person's area of influence. 2. Cor. 10:13. The color of the sphere may give you added insight into the meaning of the dream

Spider-spiders are demonic spirits; symbols of lies and confusion or a web of deceit in someone's life, Isa. 59:4-5

Spider web-a web can symbolize a trap made of lies and confusing information, Isa. 59:4-5

Spiral-a spiral staircase or spiral mountain path is symbolic of progressively moving up or down in life from one area to another

Spirit guide-a spirit guide is a demonic spirit posing as a guide to the supernatural. A spirit guide manifests itself in a dream as a talking animal or a person. Sometimes demons pose as a dead relative

Spit-to see someone spit at you in a dream is symbolic of contempt, Job 17:6

Splinter-symbolic of being angry at others over minor things, Matt. 7:5

Sports-to dream about playing sports can be symbolic of the game of life

Spring (season) symbolic of new life, Zech. 10:1

Spring rain-symbolic of the presence of God, Hosea 6:3

Springs of water-a symbol of a person's heart, Prov. 4:23. If the water is clear it symbolizes purity of speech. If the water is dirty it symbolizes deceit. Springs may also symbolize the blessing of the Lord, Deut. 8:7

Spy-a spy can be symbolic of an enemy of the righteous, Ps. 37:32. Spies are also symbolic of people who influence the opinions of other Christians over issues of church direction and ministry, Num. 13:32

Squatters-symbolic of evil spirits in possession of something without authority to be there

Staff-symbolic of power or old age, Zech. 8:1

Staggering-symbolic of being led away from the truth by a spirit of distortion, Isa. 19:14. Staggering may also symbolize being a drunk, Isa. 28:7

Stagnant water-symbolic of spiritual apathy, Zeph. 1:12

Stairs-symbolic of a step by step progression towards a goal in life

Standard-to see a banner or military standard in a dream is a sign and can be good or bad depending on what is written on the standard, Ps. 74:4. A standard is also symbolic of receiving help from God when faced with overwhelming enemies, Isa. 59:19

Stars-angels or fallen angels, Judg. 5:20, Rev. 1:20, Rev. 12:4

Statue-an idol, something you worship, Deut. 27:15

Statue of Liberty-symbolic of the United States. Also symbolic of the freedom we have in Christ to live under the law of liberty, James 1:25

Steering wheel-symbolic of control over a person's life. If the wheel is in the back seat it symbolizes someone who wants control over another person's life

Steps-to dream of steps is symbolic of moving in either the right or wrong direction. If the steps lead upward it can symbolize a hard journey. If the steps move downward it can symbolize the path to death, Prov. 5:5

Sting-symbolic of the mental torment of demonic oppressors, Num. 21:6

Stirring-symbolic of being the cause of strife, mischief or trouble, Prov. 10:12

Stock market-trusting in money or a gamble in life

Stomach-symbolic of the flesh, 1 Cor. 6:13

Stone-symbolic of Christ, Zech. 3:9. Also symbolic of hardness of heart, Ezek. 11:19

Stone face-symbolic of being hardened and unrepentant from sin, Jer. 5:3

Stone-wall-symbolic of an obstacle. If the wall is broken down it can symbolize the need to rebuild something, Prov. 24:31

Stopwatch-symbolic of being under a time constraint

Store-a symbol of variety and choices in life

Storehouse-symbolic of things that are stored but accessible only through God, Job 38:22

Stork-symbolic of following God's commands, doing what one is supposed to do, Jer. 8:7

Storm-representative of distresses in life, Ps. 107:28-29

Straight path-symbolic of ease in life, being led by God, Jer. 31:9

Strain-to filter something in a dream is symbolic of worrying about minor details rather than what is important, Matt. 23:24

Straining-being under duress, Mark 6:48

Straitjacket-symbolic of spiritual and psychological imprisonment

Strangulation-strangling yourself can be symbolic of an unsuccessful attempt to take control or move into a position of power, 2 Sam. 17:23. If you are strangling someone else it can symbolize a hatred for that person. If you are being strangled it can be a demonic dream. If you are watching someone being strangled it can be a warning about a physical or spiritual attack on that person

Straw-worthless words or valueless work, Jer. 23:28

Strawberries-symbolic of a delicacy

Stream-a stream is symbolic of life with Christ. A stream that is deep when stepped into is symbolic of life flowing from God, Ps. 65:9, Ezek. 47:5

Street-symbolic of a public area in life. A street can symbolize hypocrisy, Matt. 6:5, or evangelism, Lk.14:23

Street sign-a sign is a dream symbol designed to point you in a direction or give you a warning or a command

Stretcher-symbolic of injury or sickness, Lk.5:24

Strongman-this can be a demonic oppressor, Matt 12:29

Student-if you are a student in a dream it symbolizes a time of learning and submission in your life. If you are dreaming of being around students it can symbolize a position of authority over others, Acts 19:9

Studying-symbolic of a wearisome activity, Eccl. 12:12

Stumbling block-symbolic of causing someone to sin, Matt. 16:23

Stump (tree) symbolic of being cutoff, Job 14:8. A stump can also symbolize a godly remnant, Isa. 6:13

Stylus-symbolic of entrenched habits, Jer. 17:1

Suffocate-to dream of being suffocated may be indicative of a sleeping disorder or activity from demonic oppressors

Sugar-symbolic of telling people what they want to hear as opposed to what they need to hear, 2 Tim. 4:3

Suicide-to dream of killing yourself is symbolic of self-destructive behavior (drinking, drugging and promiscuity). To see someone else committing suicide can be a warning about that person's life

Suing-symbolic of unrighteous behavior, Matt. 5:40

Suit-symbolic of being serious and highly conscientious about what you do

Sulfur-God's judgment against the wicked, Ps. 11:6

Summer-symbolic of preparation, Prov. 6:8

Summer fruits-gladness and joy, Isa. 16:9

Sun-the sun is a reference to someone's father or Jesus. A bright shining sun is symbolic of God's goodness and fullness of life. A dark red, raging or darkened sun is emblematic of the apocalypse. The sun can also symbolize endurance, Ps. 89:36

Sun, moon and stars-symbolic of order, Jer. 31:35, or your father, mother and siblings, Gen. 37:9-10

Sunburn-symbolic of a hard worker, Song. 1:6

Sunflowers-flowers in bloom are symbolic of an awakening love, Song. 2:7-12

Sunglasses-symbolic of someone who is trying to mask their true feelings, thoughts and intentions

Sunset-peace, tranquility, praising God, Ps. 113:3

Superhero (Batman, Superman) to dream of being a superhero can symbolize your role in fighting injustice or forces of spiritual wickedness, 2 Cor. 10:4-5

Surgery-symbolic of stripping your life of unwanted things

Surrounded-if you dream of being surrounded it can symbolize being hated and slandered by other people, Ps. 109:3

Swallow (bird) symbolic of blessing, peace or finding the right place to live, Ps. 84:3

Swarms-to dream of swarming insects is symbolic of a devourer or destroyer, Ps. 78:45

Swashbuckler-a person who is difficult to live with and likes to argue, Titus 3:10

Sweeping-cleaning out your life, Isa. 14:23

Sweets-confections are symbolic of gossip, Prov. 18:8

Swift (bird) a symbol of order and obedience to God's commands, Jer. 8:7

Swimming-symbolic of your life. If you are being chased it can symbolize a spiritual enemy in your life. If you are with friends and family enjoying yourself it can symbolize fun and relaxation in life. If you are naked or topless while swimming it symbolizes a feeling of having your weaknesses exposed to other people

Swimming pool-symbolic of a gathering place for people. If the water is dirty it symbolizes that you are in a bad environment or your current situation is filled with negativity

Sword-symbolic of the word of God, Heb. 4:12. A sword is also symbolic of the Holy Spirit, Eph. 6:17. A sword can also be a warning for a person to be on guard, Lk. 22:36

Symphony-symbolic of working in perfect union with others. Also symbolic of prophesying and giving thanks to God, 1 Chron. 25:1-3

T.

T.V. (see television)

Table-symbolic of people with shared beliefs or similar interests, 1 Cor. 10:21. Sitting at a dark table is symbolic of ungodly activities in your life

Tablet-symbolic of your heart, Prov. 7:3

Tabloid-symbolic of having a morbid interest in gossip, 1 Tim. 5:13

Tail-if you dream of having a tail it can symbolize immature behavior. A tail can also symbolize being last or unimportant, Deut. 28:13. Having a tail is also symbolic of a false teacher, Isa. 9:15

Talking back-to dream of someone talking back to authority is a symbol of foolishness and rebellion, 1 Sam. 15:23, Prov. 12:1

Tall-symbolic of being important in your own eyes or the eyes of others, 1 Sam. 9:2. Being tall is also symbolic of a person of high social standing, Isa. 10:33

Tambourine-joy, praise, Ps. 81:2, Jer. 31:4

Tank-symbolic of heavy protection or having a militant attitude

Tanned-symbolic of beautifying oneself

Tapeworm-a tapeworm can be a manifestation of anxieties associated with not being able to gain weight

Tape measure-symbolic of examining someone or something, Rev. 11:1, 2 Cor. 10:12-13

Tar-symbolic of getting trapped, Gen. 14:10

Tarantula-symbolic of a sorcerer or a demonic spirit, Isa. 59:4-5

Target-symbolic of aiming at a goal in life or targeting someone for good or evil, Lam. 3:12

Tarot cards-symbolic of fortune telling, Acts 16:16

Taskmaster-symbolic of a harsh or overbearing person in a position of authority, Ex. 1:11

Tattoo-symbolic of worldliness or pagan rituals, Lev. 19:28

Tax-taxes or a tax notice is symbolic of earthly government, Matt. 17:25

Teacher-symbolic of authority, Ex. 18:20

Tears-symbolic of hurt, pain, broken heartedness and a longing for God, Ps. 42:3

Teenagers-symbolic of carelessness and youth, Job 33:25

Teeth-symbolic of a person's words. Colorful teeth symbolize someone who likes to tell fanciful stories. Cracked teeth can symbolize a fear of dying or aging. Missing teeth can symbolize not having anything to say. Your teeth falling out may symbolize a fast lifestyle, decay or fear of getting older. Sharp or razor teeth can symbolize that you use your words as weapons, Ps. 57:4. Clean teeth may symbolize not having any food or a spiritual drought, Amos 4:6. Broken teeth can symbolize anguish, mourning and bitterness in life, Lam. 3:16. Seeing teeth shatter can symbolize God fighting against your enemies, Ps. 3:7

Television-symbolic of idleness or being unproductive

Temple-a temple can be symbolic of a pagan deity or the temple of God, Ps. 27:4

Tennis-symbolic of being locked in competition against a single person, at home, on the job or in school

Tent-symbolic of a temporary living situation, Jer.14:8. An elaborate tent can symbolize the secret place of God, Ps. 27:5

Termite-tiny nuisances, things that bother you that you can't seem to fix or get rid of

Terror-symbolic of death, Ps. 55:4

Test-symbolic of measuring or examining, Gen. 22:1

Theater-to be in a theater or auditorium in a dream with dead people is symbolic of having wandered away from the truth, Prov. 21:16-17

Thief-a symbol of demonic activity around you and your family with intentions of stealing your peace, sleep, joy and love, Jn. 10:10

Thigh-a symbol of strength, Ps. 45:3

Thirst-a symbol of longing for something in your life. The sensation of thirst can symbolize a desire for God, Ps. 42:2

Thorns-a thorn is a symbol of sin, worries and cares in life, Matt. 13:7. A thorn can also symbolize the suffering of Christ on the cross, Matt. 27:29

Thread-symbolic of the smallest portion of a person's property, Gen. 14:23. A thread can also symbolize that a non-believer has decided to place their trust in Christ, Josh. 2:18

Throne-a symbol of rule, reign and sovereignty over a place or situation, Col. 1:16. A throne is also symbolic of God's supremacy, Ps. 45:6

Throwing-to hurl or throw someone is symbolic of banishment, Jer. 16:13

Thumbs-up-the "thumbs up" sign symbolizes authorization to do something

Thunder-symbolic of God's voice, Ps. 77:18

Ticket-if you dream of being written a ticket by a police officer it is symbolic of a godly warning before you suffer further consequences for your behavior

Tidal wave-symbolic of impending disaster, 2 Sam. 22:5

Tie-a neck-tie symbolizes keeping a neat and professional appearance

Tiger-for many non-Christians a tiger is symbolic of strength, good character and solitude. A tiger can also be a manifestation of a spiritual enemy in someone's life attempting to stalk and devour them

Tightrope-symbolic of trying to keep your emotions and family together during a tricky situation

Tight space-a feeling of anxiety produced by being in a small space is a reflection of a situation in life that is suffocating or difficult, Jer. 38:6

Tin-symbolic of things of little value, Ezek. 22:18

Tire-symbolic of your ability to move in life. If the tire is flat it symbolizes your inability to go anywhere

Toad-symbolic of demonic spirits, Rev. 16:13

Tobacco-symbolic of bad habits

Toilet-a symbol of exposure or needing to flush something out of your life. Going down a toilet can symbolize flushing your life away or the hard and dirty path to a new place

Tollbooth-symbolic of something that will cost you in order to move from one area in life to another

Tomb-symbolic of death or a hypocrite, Matt. 23:27

Tombstone-symbolic of death. The inscription on the tombstone will give you more insight into the meaning of the dream

Tongue-a split, cut or missing tongue is symbolic of confusion and perversion, Ps. 55:9, Prov. 10:31

Tooth (see teeth)

Toothache-symbolic of a source of constant irritation, Prov. 25:19

Toothpaste-symbolic of a need to clean up your speech, to stop cursing and complaining

Topaz-symbolic of something highly valuable in life, Job 28:19

Topless-being topless symbolizes exposure in life. If you did not feel ashamed during the dream it symbolizes being comfortable about yourself in front of people

Tornado-a tornado can be symbolic of the presence of God, Nah. 1:3. It can also be symbolic of trouble and distress in life, Ps. 107:28-29. Multiple tornadoes symbolize multiple problems. It takes spiritual discernment to determine if the tornado is God's presence or a fast-approaching problem

Torture-to see someone being tortured is symbolic of demonic torment, Rev. 9:5, Matt. 18:34

Tourist-symbolic of visiting a place in life for a short time

Tow truck-symbolic of helping other people

Towel-symbolic of service towards others, Jn. 13:4

Tower-a place of refuge, Ps. 61:3

Toy-symbolic of something regarded as unnecessary, something wanted for amusement

Track-symbolic of competing in life, 1 Cor. 9:25

Traffic-symbolic of not being able to go where you want in life as fast as you would like

Train-symbolic of going from one place to another

Trampled-the sensation or act of being trampled in a dream suggests oppression by an enemy, Ps. 56:1-2

Trampoline-symbolic of enjoying life

Translator-symbolic of making others understand or interpreting things for other people, Neh. 8:8

Trap-a symbol of a wicked scheme against you by demons or evil people, Ps. 38:12

Trapper-a deadly enemy, Ps. 91:3

Trash-worthlessness, without value, Job 20:7. Trash on someone's face symbolizes a rebuke from God, Mal. 2:3

Treasure-symbolic of God's word, Prov. 7:1

Treasure chest-symbolic of finding something that was hidden from others and contains things of great value

Tree-trees are people or nations. The church is also depicted as a tree, Dan. 4:20-22, Matt. 13:31-32. A green tree is symbolic of a prosperous person, Ps. 52:8. An uprooted tree symbolizes a false teacher or a false prophet, someone who is spiritually dead, Jude 1:12

Tree of life-symbolic of wisdom, Prov. 3:18

Tricycle-symbolic of childishness

Triple braided rope-symbolic of strength, Eccl. 4:12

Tripping-to be tripped or to trip someone in a dream symbolizes an attempt to cause someone to fail at something, Ps. 140:4

Trojan horse-symbolic of disguised danger

Troops-symbolic of war or being under siege, Mic. 5:1

Truck-this can symbolize a ministry for a Christian or a rough and rugged style of living for a non-believer

Trumpet-praise, joy, Ps. 98:6. Also symbolic of war, Amos 3:6

Tsunami-symbolic of a stressful event or tribulation in life, Ps. 107:28-29

Tug-of-war-symbolic of friendly competition between friends

Tumbleweed-destruction, the life of a wicked person, Ps. 83:13

Tumor-to dream of a cancerous tumor may be a warning to pray for healing for someone or a metaphor for unwanted habits in your life

Turban-symbolic of justice, Job 29:14

Turtle-slowness

Turtledove-affectionate love, Ps. 74:19

Tuxedo-symbolic of formality

Twins-symbolic of a double blessing, Ps. 127:3

Two cents-symbolic of a valueless opinion

U.

UFO-symbolic of heavenly visitors

Umbilical cord-symbolic of being attached to someone or something. An umbilical cord can also signify the need to detach from someone or something

Umbrella-symbolic of God's protection, Ps. 46:1. If it is raining and you do not have an umbrella it symbolizes being unprepared or unprotected

Umpire-symbolic of Christ or a person in authority

Unicycle-symbolic of moving through life awkwardly or attempting to keep your balance in a tricky situation

Uniform-symbolic of belonging to a certain group

University-symbolic of advanced learning, Acts 19:9

Urination-to dream of urinating in someone's house is symbolic of feeling as though you have lost control of your emotions or embarrassed yourself in the presence of others. To see someone urinating in your house can be symbolic of your perception of that person having committed an offensive act against you

V.

Vacuum cleaner-symbolic of needing to clean out your life

Vagrant-a vagrant symbolizes an outcast, wanderer and murderer, Gen. 4:12

Valedictorian-symbolic of being praised for performing well

Valentine-a symbol of romance

Valley-symbolic of the low points in life and the territory of the enemy, Ps. 23:4

Vampire-this is symbolic of a person who sucks the life out of you, a bad influence in your life

Van (see vehicles)

Vapor-symbolic of fleeting wealth, Prov. 21:6

V-chip-symbolic of the need to censor things from your life

Vegetable-to dream of eating vegetables may imply meekness or humble circumstances, Prov. 15:17

Vehicle (car, boat, bus, plane) symbols of ministry for a Christian. For non-believers vehicles represent the ride of life or a style of living

Veil-covering or something hidden, Song. 1:7

Venom-destructive language or activities, Ps. 58:3-4

Ventriloquist-symbolic of someone who is not in control of their life or being controlled by demonic forces

Vest-symbolic of the need for more protection

Veteran-someone who has vast experience in warfare

Veterinarian-symbolic of compassion and helping the helpless

Vice grips-symbolic of pressure and stress, Ps. 119:143 NLT

Victory-to dream of being victorious in battle is symbolic of having wise counsel in life, Prov. 24:6

Video game-to dream of being in a video game can symbolize your life. You may feel as though life is a game. Dreaming of being in a video game can also be a product of gaming for hours on end during the day

Viking-a symbol of ferocity in battle

Village-symbolic of seclusion, Song. 7:11

Vine-symbolic of Christ, Jn. 15:1. An outstretched vine can also symbolize great influence, Jer. 48:32

Vinegar-symbolic of the reproaches and slandering of the enemy, Ps. 69:21

Vineyard-symbolic of a person's life. If the vineyard is over-grown with thorns and weeds it symbolizes laziness, Prov. 24:30-31

Violin-symbolic of soothing and pleasant activities

Viper (see snakes)

Virgin-this is a Christian or the church, Matt. 25:1-10

Virgin Mary-to dream of the mother of Jesus may symbolize the Lord's favor in someone's life, Lk. 1:28. To dream of the Virgin Mary blocking your view of Christ may symbolize a need to refocus your worship upon Jesus

Vitamins-symbolic of doing things that are good for you or a symbol of needing to do things that are good for you

Voices-to hear voices in a dream is symbolic of restlessness, distractions and pressures from an enemy, Ps. 55:2-3

Volcano-a symbol of the end times or God's judgment

Volleyball-symbolic of the game of life

Vomit-rolling in vomit is symbolic of being humiliated, Jer. 48:26

Vomiting-someone vomiting in a dream is symbolic of being mentally, physically or spiritually poisoned by an environment or an ungodly influence. Eating vomit is symbolic of repeating bad behavior, Prov. 26:11

Voodoo doll-symbolic of witchcraft

Vulture-a vulgar or wicked person

W.

Wadi-a dry wadi is symbolic of hoping in things that bring disappointment, Job 6:15-20

Wagon-symbolic of carrying burdensome things or people, Amos 2:13

Waiter-a symbol of servitude

Walking-peace, tranquility, contentment in life. If two people are walking together in a dream it symbolizes complete agreement, Amos 3:3

Walking stick-symbolic of power or old age, Zech. 8:4

Wall-to dream of a wall suggests a barrier to your movement in life. To hide behind a wall in a dream symbolizes finding protection. A leaning wall is symbolic of a person under pressure, Ps. 62:3. A high, flimsy wall can symbolize the folly of trusting in wealth, Prov. 18:11. A broken wall symbolizes not having self-control, Prov. 25:28

War-to dream of war can be symbolic of the end-times, Matt. 24:6

Warehouse-symbolic of things that are stored but accessible only through God, Job 38:22-23

Warlock-if you dream of a warlock it is a sign that people influenced by Satanic religious practices have been recruited to influence a person or event, Num. 22:7

Washbowl-this is symbolic of servitude, Ps. 60:8

Washing (hands, body or feet) symbolic of cleansing from sin, Ex. 30:19-21, Ps. 26:6, Jn. 13:8

Wasp-symbolic of a spirit of terror and confusion, Ex. 23:27-28

Watchmen-a prophet or a person's legs, Eccl. 12:3

Water-symbolic of the word of God and sanctification, Eph. 5:26

Water fountain-symbolic of good words and life, Prov. 10:11

Water tower-a man-made cistern may symbolize trusting in things other than God, Jer. 2:13

Waterfall-a waterfall can be a place of peace and rest during life's journey. If the waterfall is raging it can symbolize a long climb or descent in your progress in life

Watering-symbolic of generous giving, Prov. 11:25

Waves-tumultuous people or a stormy period in your life, Ps. 65:7, Jer. 51:42. Waves are also symbolic of false doctrine, trickery and deceit, Eph. 4:14. A wave may also be symbolic of a move of the Holy Spirit

Wax-symbolic of a faint heart, Ps 22:14

Wedding-a symbol of new beginnings, joy and happiness, Matt. 25:10

Wedding cake-symbolic of matrimony and unending love

Weeds-a symbol of bad activities or bad people, Heb. 6:8

Well-a place of drawing water, symbolic of a person's spouse, Prov. 5:15. A well can also be a person's heart, Eccl. 12:6

Werewolf-symbolic of people whose actions and attitudes can turn them into a monster. A werewolf can also be a spiritual enemy

West (see directions)

Whale-symbolic of running from God or being devoured by a large problem, Jon. 1:17

Wheat-symbolic of a true believer, legitimacy or God's word, Matt. 13:24

Wheelchair-symbolic of recovery from injury or needing help

Whip-a curse, stubbornness, Prov. 26:3

Whirlwind-a whirlwind can be symbolic of God's presence, Nah. 1:3. It can also be symbolic of calamity, Prov. 1:27. If you survive the whirlwind it signifies your righteousness, Prov. 10:25

Whispering-someone or something whispering in a dream is symbolic of hateful words or enemies taking counsel against you, Ps. 41:6

Whistle-symbolic of calling someone, Isa. 5:26

White horse-symbolic of the return of Christ, Rev. 6:2

Wilderness-a place of spiritual dryness, Amos 5:25or solitude for a time of training in life, Matt. 4:1

Willow tree-weeping, mourning, sorrow, Ps. 137:2

Wind-symbolic of the Holy Spirit, Acts 2:2. A stormy or scorching wind is symbolic of troubles, Ps. 55:8, Jer. 4:11-12

Window-symbolic of vision, insight or a person's eyes, Eccl. 12:3

Wine-a symbol of Christ's blood and the forgiveness of sins, Matt. 26:28

Winged women-symbolic of an order of angelic beings, Zech. 5:9

Wings-symbolic of freedom and rest from trouble, Ps. 55:6. Wings also symbolize swift movement, Jer. 48:9

Wink-symbolic of a gesture of approval or acknowledgment

Winnowing-symbolic of cleansing and revival, Jer. 4:11

Winter-symbolic of peace, tranquility or a late stage in a person's life

Wisdom-symbolic of riches, honor, peace and long life, Prov. 3:16-17

Witch-symbolic of a person involved with the Occult, Deut. 18:10

Withered-a symbol of a curse or a dying person, Ps. 37:35-36

Wolf-symbolic of a vicious person or a spiritual enemy, Ezek. 22:27, Matt. 10:16

Woman-symbolic of a helper, Gen. 2:18. A loud woman is symbolic of unwise living, Prov. 9:13. A woman in dark clothing is symbolic of a spiritual enemy, Matt. 13:33. A woman clothed in purple is symbolic of a good wife, Prov. 31:22

Woodpecker-a nuisance

Woods-the woods can be symbolic of being lost, alone or isolated from people

Wool-angel hair, purity of living, Isa. 1:18

Working-profit, Prov. 14:23

Worm-symbolic of disgrace, contempt and repugnance, Ps. 22:6

Wormwood-symbolic of bitterness, Jer. 9:15

Wound-symbolic of unconfessed sin in a person's life, Ps. 38:5, Jer. 30:12. A wound can be an emotional injury caused by another person that has not healed

Wreath-a symbol of teaching and instruction from wise parents, Prov. 1:8

Wrestler-to be a wrestler is symbolic of a struggle between people or spiritual powers, Gen. 30:8

Wrestling-to dream of being locked in a wrestling match is symbolic of a struggle against spiritual powers, Eph. 6:12

Wristwatch-symbolic of clock watching. If you keep checking your watch in a dream it can symbolize anxiety over an issue, 2 Pet. 3:9

Writing-to dream of writing a letter is symbolic of expressing something that you never had the chance to say to a friend or loved one

X.

X-the letter "X" or a marking in the shape of an "X" is symbolic of an area of significance or of interest. An "X" can symbolize hidden treasures (earthly or spiritual)

Xerox machine-symbolic of copying someone's behavior

X-ray-to see a medical x-ray is symbolic of having keen insight or awareness about an issue. To have x-ray vision is symbolic of having a spiritual perception to see people's true intentions in a situation, Neh. 6:12

Y.

Yard-a yard is symbolic of home-life

Yarn-a symbol of good deeds towards others, Acts 9:39

Yawing-symbolic of boredom

Yearbook-symbolic of reviewing your life's actions

Yeast-symbolic of hypocrisy, Matt. 16:6

Yelling-symbolic of a nuisance, Prov. 27:14

Yield-a yield sign is symbolic of needing to submit to authority, 1 Pet. 2:13

Yin-Yang-symbolic of someone who is influenced by Asian philosophies, Isa. 2:6

Yoga-a person doing yoga is symbolic of meditation or Hindu beliefs

Yogurt-symbolic of trying to live healthfully

Yoke-symbolic of slavery or bondage, Jer. 27:8. The work of the church, Phil. 4:3. Christ's mastery over your life, Matt. 11:29-30. To dream of a yoke may also symbolize a need to submit to authority, Lam. 3:27

Yo-Yo-symbolic of emotional ups and downs

Z.

Zealot-symbolic of someone who has an intense fervor and drive for a cause, Matt. 10:4

Zebra-symbolic of an unambiguous issue. Something that is clearly right or wrong

Zeppelin-symbolic of an impending disaster

Zero-to dream of a zero is symbolic of the absence of value

Ziggurat (Babylonian temple) symbolic of pagan worship or man's arrogance, Gen. 11:3-9

Zinc (sunscreen) symbolic of the need for protection

Zion-the golden city of God, Isa. 28:16

Zodiac signs-symbolic of mythology and predicting the future, Jer. 10:2-3

Zombies-the walking dead are symbolic of the unsaved (the people of the world are dead in their trespasses and sins) Eph. 2:1-5

Zoo-representative of a busy and active place in life

Colors

Black-a figure in black is almost always an enemy. Black skies and dark surroundings indicate your mood or the spiritual atmosphere of an area. Black is also symbolic of famine, Rev. 6:5

Blue-blue was the dominant color of the robes worn by Israel's high priest, Ex. 28. Blue is symbolic of wisdom. Dream entities with dark blue eyes or dark blue colored skin can be demonic

Bronze-symbolic of strength, Micah 4:13

Brown-symbolic of earthly wisdom. Brown can also symbolize decay, Ezek. 47:12 NLT

Copper-symbolic of low monetary value and high utility, Deut. 8:9, Mk. 12:42

Gold-symbolic of wisdom and high quality ministerial work, 1Cor. 3:12

Green-green means flourishing or life, Prov. 11:28

Grey-grey is symbolic of death, Rev. 6:8

Neon-neon colors are symbolic of attracting attention

Orange-connotative of earthly qualities. Orange can also symbolize danger

Pink-love

Purple-royalty, Lam. 4:5

Red-symbolic of rage, Isa. 63:2-3. Red can also symbolize war, Rev. 6:4

Scarlet-symbolic of the blood of Christ. Scarlet can also be symbolic of sin in someone's life, Isa. 1:18

Silver-symbolic of the word of God, Ps. 12:6. Silver can also symbolize ministry, 1Cor. 3:12

White-symbolic of righteousness, Rev. 3:5

Yellow-the word yellow means shining or gleaming. Yellow refers to something of high value